THE LITTLE RED BOOK OF

NEW YORK WISDOM

THE LITTLE RED BOOK OF
NEW YORK WISDOM

FORMER MAYOR ED KOCH

WITH GREGG STEBBEN
FOREWORD BY PAT FARNACK

Skyhorse Publishing

Skyhorse Publishing books may be purchased in bulk at special discounts for sales promotion, corporate gifts, fund-raising, or educational purposes. Special editions can also be created to specifications. For details, contact the Special Sales Department, Skyhorse Publishing, 307 West 36th Street, 11th Floor, New York, NY 10018 or info@skyhorsepublishing.com.

Skyhorse® and Skyhorse Publishing® are registered trademarks of Skyhorse Publishing, Inc.®, a Delaware corporation.

www.skyhorsepublishing.com

10 9 8 7 6 5 4 3 2 1

Library of Congress Cataloging-in-Publication Data is available on file.

Cover design by Adam Bozarth

ISBN: 978-1-5107-2560-7

Printed in China

Contents

Foreword

Y ou might find it strange that a girl with her roots in rural Pennsylvania would identify so strongly with *The Little Red Book of New York Wisdom*. But, from a very young age, my heart and mind belonged in New York City.

It's always been this way, dating back to my earliest subway ride as an eight-year-old, holding my father's hand tightly while trying to appear to be a grown up, navigating the big bad city, entirely on my own.

The magic of Rockefeller Center at Christmas or the mystery of a long and somber Latin mass with its incense and hypnotic chanting at the achingly beautiful St. Patrick's Cathedral. The excitement of picking up exotic overseas relatives at Idlewild Airport. Even now, I wonder: Were these dreams or did they really happen?

I knew New York was where the action was, the talent, the glamour, the best-of-the-best. It was losing yourself in the roar of the grease paint, sitting right up front by the stage, almost close enough to count the actor's pores, or hurrying past those who are down on their luck, at the bus terminal or in Times Square. But even as a wide-eyed child, I knew with a certainty I never questioned that I would be part of it all, one day.

New York may annoy and infuriate you at times, but, to me, it's like a loud and obnoxious friend who you can never quite bring yourself to leave for too long.

Which brings me to the one-of-a-kind Ed Koch, who loved being on the streets of New York, just as much as I have. I will close with these words of wisdom from the young Ed "How-Am-I-Doing" Koch while he was still a member of Congress, before he was "Da Mayor" of New York City: "I cannot justify approving monies to find out whether or not there is some microbe on Mars, when I KNOW, in fact, there are rats in Harlem apartments."

I hope you enjoy this book and all its words of New York wisdom, as much as I have. And I hope you also enjoy every minute you ever spend in NYC!

Pat Farnack
WCBS Midday Host
June 2017

Introduction

The Little Red Book of New York Wisdom is powerful stuff. Everyone who writes, even an occasional speech or a stylish letter, should have it available. Why? Because it includes hundreds of bright sayings by political figures who include Bella Abzug and myself. The editors included three of my best quotes and seven of Woody Allen's. Those quoted in the book include public officials, writers, playwrights, movie makers, philosophers, and so many more.

New York City is special. Why? Because less than half of its residents were actually born here. I'm one of them, born in the Bronx in 1924. The majority come from every country in the world; from every state in the Union. We have the ablest and most courageous people in the world and their store of knowledge—wisdom—is extraordinary.

Let me now give you two more phrases of wisdom. One's mine and the other's that of F. Scott Fitzgerald, who wrote one of the most long lasting books about New York City and its environs, *The Great Gatsby*. My quote was uttered in 1990 after the Democratic primary when I lost to David Dinkins and he was elected in the general election. The following year, many were urging me to run again. I replied, "No, the people threw me out, and now the people must be punished." Fitzgerald wrote of the Queensboro Bridge (which starts in Manhattan at 59th Street and 2nd Avenue and ends in Long Island City, Queens), "The City seen from the Queensboro Bridge is always the City seen for the first time, in its first wild promise of all the mystery and the beauty in the world."

Why does that brilliant statement mean so much to me? Mayor Michael Bloomberg and the New York City Council renamed the bridge the Ed Koch-Queensboro Bridge. Now you understand.

I am looking for an off-the-shelf canvas cover for the bridge to protect it when it rains so it won't rust. Anyone out there know where I can buy one?

Edward I. Koch
June 9, 2011

PART ONE

Quotable New York

New York is to the nation what the white church spire is to the village—the visible symbol of aspiration and faith, the white plume saying the way is up.
E. B. WHITE, "MENTAL HEALTH IN THE METROPOLIS"

• • •

New York is the place where all the aspirations of the Western World meet to form one vast master aspiration, as powerful as the suction of a steam dredge. It is the icing on the pie called Christian civilization.
H. L. MENCKEN, *PREJUDICES, SIXTH SERIES,* 1927

• • •

The whole world revolves around New York. Very little happens anywhere unless someone in New York presses the button.
DUKE ELLINGTON

• • •

New York is the only real city-city.
TRUMAN CAPOTE

• • •

When Wall Street sneezes, the rest of the world catches a cold.
ANONYMOUS

• • •

I'd rather be a lamppost in New York than the mayor of Chicago.
JIMMY WALKER, MAYOR, 1926–1932

• • •

Something's always happening here. If you're bored in New York it's your own fault.
MYRNA LOY

• • •

New York attracts the most talented people in the world in
the arts and professions. It also attracts them in other fields.
Even the bums are talented.
EDMUND LOVE, *SUBWAYS ARE FOR SLEEPING*

• • •

He speaks English with the flawless imperfection of a
New Yorker.
GILBERT MILLSTEIN

• • •

One belongs to New York instantly. One belongs to it as
much in five minutes as in five years.
THOMAS WOLFE, *THE WEB AND THE ROCK,* 1939

• • •

Manhattan is a machine, fueled by the millions of people
who pour through its streets and subways each day, many of
them locked in an exhausting but addictive lifestyle which
makes anywhere else seem dull and slow.
FIONA DUNCAN AND LEONIE GLASS

• • •

Everyone in New York knows that he is an important person
living among other important persons.
BRENDAN BEHAN, "WHERE WE ALL CAME INTO
TOWN,"*EVERGREEN REVIEW*

• • •

There are only about 400 people in fashionable New York
society. If you go outside the number, you strike people who
are either not at ease in a ballroom, or make other people
not at ease. See the point?
WARD MCCALLISTER

• • •

The crime problem in New York is getting really serious. The
other day the Statue of Liberty had both hands up.
JAY LENO

• • •

Other cities consume culture, New York creates it.
PAUL GOLDBERGER, *THE CITY OBSERVED*

• • •

New York is where the future comes to audition.
ED KOCH, MAYOR, 1978–1989

• • •

New York, the nation's thyroid.
CHRISTOPHER MORLEY, *SHORE LEAVE*

• • •

The capital city of high-tension activity.
STANLEY LEVEY

• • •

New York now leads the world's great cities in the number of
people around whom you shouldn't make a sudden move.
DAVID LETTERMAN

• • •

New York has a
trip-hammer vitality which drives you insane with
restlessness, if you have no inner stabiliser.
HENRY MILLER, *THE COLOSSUS OF MAROUSSI,* 1941

• • •

The great days in New York were just before you got there.
LEWIS GANNETT, *COUNTRY JOURNAL*

• • •

She dreamed, lulled by the train, of getting off at heaven or
New York City, whichever she got to first.
MARY LEE SETTLE

• • •

To step from a train platform into Grand Central's
extraordinary concourse . . . is to feel in every fiber that you
have arrived someplace important, to know that you have
come into a great city and that great city has greeted you
properly.
PAUL GOLDBERGER

• • •

New York is one of the finest cities I ever saw . . . . Situated
on an island, which I think it will one day cover, it rises, like
Venice from the sea, and receives into its lap tribute of all
the riches of the earth.
FRANCES TROLLOPE, *DOMESTIC MANNERS OF THE
AMERICANS*

• • •

What else can you expect from a town that's shut off from the world by the ocean on one side and New Jersey on the other?
O. HENRY, "A TEMPERED WIND," *THE GENTLE GRAFTER*

• • •

A little strip of an island with a row of well-fed folks up and down the middle, and a lot of hungry folks on each side.
HARRY LEON WILSON, *THE SPENDERS,* 1902

• • •

The only credential the city asked was the boldness to dream. For those who did, it unlocked its gates and its treasures, not caring who they were or where they came from.
MOSS HART, *ACT ONE,* 1959

• • •

Here I was in New York, city of prose and fantasy, of capitalist automation, its streets a triumph of cubism, its moral philosophy that of the dollar. New York impressed me tremendously because, more than any other city in the world, it is the fullest expression of our modern age.
LEON TROTSKY, *MY LIFE,* 1930

• • •

Little has changed in our New York neighborhoods except the faces, the names, and the languages spoken. The same decent values of hard work and accomplishment and service to city and nation still exist.
DAVID DINKINS, MAYOR, 1990–1993

• • •

I think that New York is not the cultural center of America, but the business and administrative center of American culture.
SAUL BELLOW, IN A RADIO INTERVIEW, 1969

• • •

Every great wave of popular passion that rolls up on the prairies is dashed to spray when it strikes the hard rocks of Manhattan.
H. L. MENCKEN, *PREJUDICES, FOURTH SERIES,* 1925

• • •

To say that New York came up to its advance billing would be the baldest of understatements. Being there was like being in heaven without going to all the bother and expense of dying.
P. G. WODEHOUSE, *AMERICA, I LIKE YOU*

• • •

The present in New York is so powerful that the past is lost.
JOHN JAY CHAPMAN, LETTER, MARCH 26, 1898

• • •

The alive, pulsing city is the greatest artistic achievement of humankind.
DR. JAMES HILLMAN

• • •

New York has a life of its own, its own pulse, which beats just a bit faster than that of its inhabitants.
URI SAVIR, ISRAELI CONSUL GENERAL

• • •

New York is like disco, but without the music.
ELAINE STRITCH, QUOTED OBSERVER

• • •

New York's a small place when it comes to the part of it that wakes up just as the rest is going to bed.
P. G. WODEHOUSE,
THE AUNT AND THE SLUGGARD

• • •

New York is great though. If you're here and want a one of a kind souvenir be sure to take home the police sketch of your assailant.
DAVID LETTERMAN

• • •

Crazed with avarice, lust and rum,
New York, thy name's Delirium.
B. R. NEWTON, "OWED TO NEW YORK"

• • •

New York was no mere city. It was instead an infinitely
romantic notion, the mysterious nexus of all love and money
and power, the shining and perishable dream itself. To
think of "living" there was to reduce the miraculous to the
mundane; one does not "live" at Xanadu.
JOAN DIDION, *SLOUCHING TOWARDS BETHLEHEM*

• • •

"I was in love with New York. I do not mean 'love' in any
colloquial way, I mean that I was in love with the city, the
way you love the first person who ever touches you and
never love anyone quite that way again."
JOAN DIDION, *SLOUCHING TOWARDS BETHLEHEM*

• • •

The beautiful city, the city of hurried and sparkling waters!
The city of spires and masts!
The City nested in bays! My city! The city of such women, I
as mad with them! I will return after death to be with them!
The city of such young men, I swear I cannot live happy
without I often go talk, walk, eat, drink, sleep with them!
WALT WHITMAN, *LEAVES OF GRASS,* 1900

• • •

I miss the animal buoyancy of New York, the animal vitality.
I did not mind that it had no meaning and no depth.
ANAlS NIN, *DIARIES,* VOL. 2

• • •

There is a great tango of eye contact between men and
women on the streets of New York.
JOSEPH GIOVANNI

• • •

New York is an exciting town where something is happening
all the time, most of it unsolved.
JOHNNY CARSON

• • •

The great big city's a wondrous toy
Just made for a girl and boy
We'll turn Manhattan
Into an isle of joy.
LORENZ HART, "MANHATTAN," 1925

• • •

This is the province of let's pretend located in the
state of anomie.
GAIL SHEEHY, *HUSTLING*

• • •

New York, thy name is irreverence and hyperbole.
And grandeur.
ADA LOUISE HUXTABLE, *NEW YORK TIMES*
ARCHITECTURE CRITIC

• • •

The pavements of New York are filled with people escaping the prison sentence of personal history into the promise of an open destiny.
VIVIAN GORNICK, THE *NEW YORKER*

• • •

The lusts of the flesh can be gratified anywhere; it is not this sort of license that distinguishes New York. It is, rather, a lust of the total ego for recognition, even for eminence. More than elsewhere, everybody here wants to be somebody.
SYDNEY J. HARRIS

• • •

There are two million interesting people in New York—and only seventy-eight in Los Angeles.
NEIL SIMON

• • •

Robinson Crusoe, the self-sufficient man, could not have lived in New York City.
WALTER LIPPMAN

• • •

People say New Yorkers can't get along. Not true. I saw two
New Yorkers, complete strangers, sharing a cab. One guy
took the tires and the radio; the other guy took the engine.
DAVID LETTERMAN

• • •

Ah! Some love Paris,
And some love Perdue.
But love is an archer with a low IQ.
A bold, bad bowman, and innocent of pity.
So I'm in love with
New York City.
PHYLLIS MCGINLEY

• • •

If Paris is the setting for a romance, New York is the perfect
city in which to get over one, to get over anything. Here the
lost *douceur de vivre* is forgotten and the intoxication of
living takes over.
CYRIL CONNOLLY

• • •

I spend my summers in Europe and when they ask me if I'm an American, I say, "No, I'm a New Yorker."
ALEXANDER ALLAND JR.

• • •

It's not so much that I'm an American. I'm a New Yorker.
NETHERLANDS-BORN WILLIAM DE KOONING

• • •

When it's three o' clock in New York, it's still 1938 in London.
ATTRIBUTED TO BETTE MIDLER

• • •

The networks don't recognize a story until it's in the *New York Times.*
JACK ANDERSON

• • •

When an American stays away from New York too long, something happens to him. Perhaps he becomes a little provincial, a little dead, a little afraid.
SHERWOOOD ANDERSON

• • •

Toronto is kind of New York operated by the Swiss.
JOHN BENTLY MAYS

• • •

New York is the meeting place of the peoples, the only city
where you can hardly find a typical American.
DJUNA BARNES

• • •

No matter how many times I visit this great city I'm always
struck by the same thing: a yellow taxi cab.
SCOTT ADAMS

• • •

New York is a different country. Maybe it ought to have a
separate government. Everybody thinks differently, acts
differently. They just don't know what the hell the rest of the
United States is.
HENRY FORD

• • •

New York has total depth in every area. Washington has only
politics; after that, the second biggest thing is white marble.
JOHN LINDSAY, MAYOR, 1966–1973

• • •

If 1,668,172 people are to be set down in one narrow strip
of land between two quiet rivers, you can hardly improve
on this solid mass of buildings and the teeming organism of
human life that streams through them. For better or worse,
this is real.
BROOKS ATKINSON

• • •

New York means many different things to me. It certainly
means cheesecake, more species of cheesecake than I ever
knew existed: rum, orange, hazelnut, chocolate marble,
Italian, Boston, and of course, New York.
DAVID FROST

• • •

It's a city where everyone mutinies but no one deserts.
HARRY HERSHFIELD

• • •

What is barely hinted at in other American cities is
condensed and enlarged in New York.
SAUL BELLOW

• • •

Personally, I've always favored New York 'cause this is one
city where you don't have to ride in the back of the bus. Not
that they're so liberal—it's just that in New York, nobody
moves to the back of the bus.
DICK GREGORY, *FROM THE BACK* OF *THE BUS*

• • •

New York is the city of brotherly shove.
ANONYMOUS

• • •

Every person on the streets of New York is a type. The city is
one big theater where everyone is on display.
JERRY RUBIN

• • •

New York City is all about sex. People getting it, people trying to get it, people who can't get it. No wonder the city never sleeps. It's too busy trying to get laid.
CARRIE BRADSHAW, *SEX AND THE CITY*

• • •

I loved every single movie that was set in New York, every movie that began high above the New York skyline and moved in, every detective story, every romantic comedy, every movie about nightclubs in New York or penthouses.
WOODY ALLEN

• • •

For there is gaiety in this sprawling metropolis. You hear it in the cheep of sparrows in the park, the laughter of children in playgrounds. The banter of taxi drivers lightly insulting other motorists, and it is a truer gaiety than that which glitters in the night.
SISTER MARYANNA OF THE DOMINICAN ACADEMY

• • •

East side, west side, all around the town,
The tots sang ring-a-rosie, London Bridge is falling down;
Boys and girls together, me and Mamie O'Rourke,
Tripped the light fantastic on the sidewalks of New York.
JAMES W. BLAKE

• • •

The New York chapter of the Ku Klux Klan held a rally in downtown Manhattan earlier today after a judge ruled this week that the city could not bar the march. New Yorkers responded to the ruling as expected: Within minutes of the judge's decision, sidewalk vendors were out selling counterfeit white hoods.
COLIN QUINN, *SATURDAY NIGHT LIVE*

• • •

Manhattan crowds with their turbulent musical chorus! Manhattan faces and eyes forever for me.
WALT WHITMAN, *LEAVES OF GRASS,* 1900

• • •

I would rather see the old reservoir on 42nd street or the original Madison Square Garden than I would any of the lost wonders of the ancient world.
LOUIS AUCHINCLOSS

• • •

If I live in New York, it is because I choose to live here. It is the city of total intensity, the city of the moment.
DIANE VREELAND

• • •

New York is an ugly city; a dirty city. Its climate is a scandal, its politics are used to frighten children, its traffic is madness, its competition is murderous. But once you have lived in New York and it has become your home no place else is good enough!
JOHN STEINBECK, "THE MAKING OF NEW YORK"

• • •

My favorite city in the world is New York. Sure it's dirty— but like a beautiful lady smoking a cigar.
JOAN RIVERS

• • •

Is "New York" the most beautiful city in the world? It is not far from it. No urban nights are like the nights there. I have looked down across the city from high windows. It is then that the great buildings lose reality and take on magical powers.
EZRA POUND

• • •

I've occasionally remarked that I can't imagine living anywhere other than New York or doing anything other than writing. But how could that be true? Imagination is a writer's stock in trade.
LAWRENCE BLOCK

• • •

As soon as you feel you understand New York, an unpalatable fact becomes apparent: your understanding is obsolete.
JOHN GATTUSO

• • •

Any attempt to define New York today recalls the Zen wisdom that you can't step in the same stream twice. The city is mutable, so constantly changing that it's almost impossible to get a fix on it. . . . Simply put, New York never gets boring. Anything can happen here.
CHERYL FARR LEAS

• • •

New York meets the most severe test that may be applied to the definition of a metropolis—it stays up all night. But also it becomes a small town when it rains.
JOHN GUNTHER

• • •

A haven as cosy as toast . . .
DYLAN THOMAS

• • •

New York City is considering doubling its cigarette tax, which would make a pack of cigarettes almost nine dollars. Replied the smokers, "Oh my god that's outrageous. Alright we'll pay it."
AMY POEHLER, *SATURDAY NIGHT LIVE*

• • •

New York will be a great place if they ever finish it.
O. HENRY

• • •

There have been many days in New York when I was running for mayor, and then since I've been mayor, when I would have a weekend in which I would go to a mosque on Friday; a synagogue on Saturday, and a church-sometimes two churches-on a Sunday. And by the time I finished, I would say to myself, "I know that we're getting through to God." We're talking to him in every language that He understands.
RUDOLPH W. GIULIANI

PART TWO

• • •

Only in New York

If you ever had a desire to serve on a jury, I can assure you,
professionally and personally, this will be a good one.
CHARLES SOLOMON, NEW YORK STATE SUPREME
COURT JUSTICE, TO PROSPECTIVE JURORS FOR THE
PUFF DADDY TRIAL

• • •

When he came into the great dining room at dinner time,
and looked at all the tables thronged with members of the
legislature and the lobby he never doubted that he could buy
every man in the room if he were willing to pay the price.
GEORGE WILLIAM CURTIS, ON BOSS TWEED

• • •

One month after New York City began a test of six new sidewalk toilets, going to the bathroom has become New York's latest tourist attraction.
JONATHON RABINOWITZ, REPORTER, THE *NEW YORK TIMES*

• • •

We had one toilet for everyone on the floor. And I would sit for hours in the toilet and read Shakespeare. One girl would knock on the door and say, "Hey, Shakespeare, get out of there."
WALTER MATTHAU

• • •

At the beginning my wan face was seen at a few cocktail parties, and people would come up and say, "I hear you're right down the toilet." I dreaded going out, and I dreaded going home to the tacky apartment I had rented, with disgusting leopard-skin sofas.
TINA BROWN, *VANITY FAIR,* THEN *NEW YORKER* EDITOR

• • •

I was rehabilitating this brownstone—when was it? Six
years ago? Suddenly it came back to me. I'm an obsessive-
compulsive! Back in the late twenties I worked in Palestine.
And now I'm doing it all over again on the West Side—
reclaiming ancient Jewish land.
MEYER LEVIN

• • •

As a New York cop, you'll be faced with many decisions. . . .
Do I turn this evidence in to the precinct and get it off of the
street, or do I sell it on the black market and
pocket the money?
BRIAN CLARKE

• • •

It was Christmas Eve and I had a severe gall bladder attack.
I had to take a cab to the [hospital], got out, and fell into
the gutter. There I was, lying there, thinking, "Here I am a
published writer, and I am dying like a dog." That's when I
decided I would be rich and famous.
MARIO PUZO, AUTHOR, *THE GODFATHER*

• • •

The traditional pedestrian's right of way is, as Shakespeare says, "more honored in the breach than the observance." New Yorkers pay no attention whatsoever to WALK-DON'T WALK signs (it is just a part of that New York state of mind that asks: Why trust a sign? I have eyes!)
THE NEW YORK TIMES GUIDE TO NEW YORK CITY

• • •

Visitors to New York will find that both exercise and excitement may be had at a minimum of expense through the simple practice of jay walking. With only a little experience, they may actually compete on even terms with the native New Yorker.
SIC SPAETH, *THE ADVANTAGES OF JAY WALKING,* 1926

• • •

Traffic signals in New York are just rough guidelines.
DAVID LETTERMAN

• • •

Only in New York

There are 12,000 licensed yellow taxis in New York City, and
none appear to pick up fares in the rain.
FIONA DUNCAN AND LEONIE GLASS

• • •

Some of our worst congestion is caused by people in
$30,000 autos driving to $100,000-a-year jobs who leave an
expressway to save $2.
ROSS SANDLER, NYC TRANSPORTATION
COMMISSIONER, 1987

• • •

I read big fat *Les Miserables* for weeks while I took the IRT
subway for my Wednesday allergy shots. I needed to know
Jean Valjean lived a more miserable life than I did.
E. L. DOCTOROW, *LIVES OF THE POETS*

• • •

Well, Harry, are we wealthy or not?
CLARE BOOTH LUCE, TO HER HUSBAND, AFTER HE
QUESTIONED HER ABOUT A $7,000 LINGERIE BILL

• • •

I used to see Mrs. Astor in her carriage, and she looked like a very silly woman to me. There were stories about her, that once she got on a bus and the driver passed the fare box to her. She said, "No thank you, I have my own charities."
MISS CORDELIA DEAL

• • •

An English visitor had been surprised to see none other than John Jacob Astor remove his chewing tobacco from his mouth and absent-mindedly trace a watery design with it on the windowpane.
STEPHEN BIRMINGHAM, *LIFE AT THE DAKOTA*

• • •

My dad was the town drunk. Most of the time that's not so bad; but New York City?
HENRY YOUNGMAN

• • •

New York is baffling in the [sense that] it's a city that prides itself on being an absolute shithole. It's like—there's nothing good here, people are proud of that, they're happy, 'Oh, it's overpriced, and it's overpopulated, and it stinks like piss, and comics!—comics film specials here!' And they all open with a joke about, 'Yeah, you spend 8 thousand dollars a month for 9 square feet!' And you go, 'Well, why do you fucking live here?' Why do people stay here?.. But unfortunately, this is where comedy works—where people are the most miserable.
DOUG STANHOPE, *NO REFUNDS*

• • •

The rising generation of young elegants in America are particularly requested to observe that, in polished society, it is not quite *comme il faut* for gentlemen to blow their noses with their fingers, especially when in the street.
19TH-CENTURY ETIQUETTE BOOK, CIRCA 1880

• • •

When a socialist harangued Andrew Carnegie about redistribution of wealth, Carnegie asked for his secretary for two numbers—the world's population and the value of all his assets. He divided the latter by the former, then said to his secretary, "Give this man 16 cents. That is his share of my net worth."
GEORGE WILL

• • •

New York has always been going to hell but somehow it never gets there.
ROBERT M. PIRSIG

• • •

I'll never do that again.
GRETE WAITZ, ON FIRST RUNNING THE NYC MARATHON IN 1978

• • •

At the premiere of a documentary film about de Kooning, the film's narrator, Dustin Hoffman, mentioned an astronomical price brought at auction for a de Kooning painting. To the amazement of the audience, the artist's distinctive voice, marked by his flavorful Dutch accent, rose in the dark and still theater: "Jesus Christ!"
BENNETT SCHIFF

• • •

I've always loved decorating houses, my homes. And people say I have a knack for it. It's extremely demanding. I like to create the unexpected. If it's New York, I like to make a bedroom into a greenhouse. If it's London, I like to do something so exotic you don't notice the climate.
LEE RADZIWILL

• • •

I won the Italian of the Year twice in New York. I kept saying, "You don't understand. I can't accept this!"
JAMES CAAN, ON *THE GODFATHER* CONNECTION

• • •

The summer of the [Son of Sam] killings was also one of the hottest ever on record in New York. Studio 54 had just opened, Plato's Retreat was in full swing, the punk scene was happening at CBGB's; and in addition, it was Reggie Jackson's first year with the Yankees.
SPIKE LEE

• • •

The last time anybody made a list of the top hundred character attributes of New Yorkers, common sense snuck in at number 79.
DOUGLAS ADAMS, *MOSTLY HARMLESS*

• • •

I met Billie Holiday when I was five. Miss Billie called me Mister Billy. The first blind man I ever saw was W. C. Handy. My father used to bring home jazz musicians at Passover. We had swinging seders.
BILLY CRYSTAL

• • •

My parents were on the conservative side. I was the last one to wear lipstick or a bra. But there was this little quirk of smoking grass. Not every night at dinner did we sit around and get stoned. On Passover, say, somebody would light a joint and we'd all sit and smoke it.
ELLEN BARKIN

• • •

I'd sit on his lap and watch. I was sitting there one night, when he put aside his work and taught me how to touch type. I was only six, but I took to it immediately and performed for him from time to time.
CHRIS BUCKLEY, ON A LESSON FROM HIS FATHER, WILLIAM F. BUCKLEY

• • •

It's essentially doing stand-up, but it's a little bit more interesting. Plus, the audience isn't drunk. I speak free to the Democrats and charge the Republicans. I've been hired by groups that say, "We're 95 percent Republican, so we want Al Franken, and we want him to shit all over the Republicans." And I basically do.
AL FRANKEN

• • •

There is a marvelous peace in not publishing. Publishing is a
terrible invasion of my privacy. I like to write. I love to write.
But I write just for myself and my own pleasure.
J. D. SALINGER

• • •

That *New York Journal-American* was a paper where, believe
me, ya couldn't even believe the weather report.
JIMMY BRESLIN

• • •

I would give the greatest sunset in the world for one sight of
New York's skyline.
AYN RAND, *THE FOUNTAINHEAD*

• • •

Send dead roses. Dial 1-800-439-HATE and send someone
special the first thing they really deserve!
AD IN *NEW YORK* MAGAZINE

• • •

What makes New York so dreadful, I believe, is mainly the fact that the vast majority of its people have been forced to rid themselves of one of the oldest and most powerful of human instincts—the instinct to make a permanent home.
H. L. MENCKEN, *A SECOND MENCKEN CHRESTOMATHY: A NEW SELECTION FROM THE WRITINGS OF AMERICA'S LEGENDARY EDITOR, CRITIC, AND WIT*

• • •

It is an art form to hate New York City properly. So far I have always been a featherweight debunker of New York; it takes too much energy and endurance to record the infinite number of ways the city offends me.
PAT CONROY, *THE PRINCE OF TIDES*

• • •

New York was a city where men made such incredible fortunes that a new word, 'millionaire,' was on everybody's lips.
LLOYD R. MORRIS, *INCREDIBLE NEW YORK*

• • •

The city of right angles and tough, damaged people.
PETE HAMILL

• • •

This is New York, a combat zone, and everyone has to have an angle or they're not allowed over the bridges or through the tunnels. Let them have their angles, it's what they live for. You got better things to worry about, like making sure the people that actually matter don't try any funny stuff.
CYNTHIA HEIMEL

• • •

The faces in New York remind me of people who played a game and lost.
MURRAY KEMPTON

• • •

A hundred times have I thought New York is a catastrophe, and fifty times: It is a beautiful catastrophe.
LE CORBUSIER

• • •

My one thought is to get out of New York, to experience something genuinely American.
HENRY MILLER

• • •

A New Yorker is a person with an almost inordinate interest in mental health, which is only natural considering how much of that it takes to live here.
THE *NEW YORK TIMES*

• • •

That's the New York thing, isn't it. People who seem absolutely crazy going around telling you how crazy they used to be before they had therapy.
JUDITH ROSSNER

• • •

New York has more hermits than will be found in all the forests, mountains and deserts of the United States.
SIMEON STRUNSKY

• • •

New York is a great city to live in if you can afford to get out of it.
WILLIAM COLE, 1992

• • •

All of New York City is in the holiday spirit. Here's an example. I ran into a mugger and he let me go as long as I promised to write him a check.
DAVID LETTERMAN

PART THREE

• • •

Street Scenes

At three o' clock in the morning, when the rest of the city
is silent and dark, you can come suddenly on a little area
as vivacious as a country fair. In one bar, there is a little
hunchback who struts in proudly every evening, and is
petted by everyone, given free drinks, and treated as a sort of
mascot.
CARSON MCCULLERS, "BROOKLYN IS MY
NEIGHBORHOOD," *VOGUE*, 1941

• • •

New York had all the iridescence of the beginning of the world. The returning troops marched up Fifth Avenue and the girls were instinctively drawn east and north toward them—this was the greatest nation and there was gala in the air . . . whooping up our first after-the-war reunion.
F. SCOTT FITZGERALD, *THE CRACK-UP*

• • •

Across the zinc water to the tall walls, the birchlike cluster of downtown buildings shimmered up the rosy morning like a sound of horns through a chocolate brown haze. . . . Crammed on the narrow island the million windowed buildings will jut, glittering pyramid on pyramid.
JOHN DOS PASSOS, *MANHATTAN TRANSFER*

• • •

Harbors reveal a city's power, its lust for money and filth, but strangely through the haze what I distinguished first was the lone mellow promise of an island, tender retreat from straight lines . . .
DON DELILLO, *GREAT JONES STREET*

• • •

The metaphor that many first-time Visitors have employed
is of the steam which rises from manholes at some street
corners—part of an underground heating system for older
buildings. They see this as a symbol of the city's
latent energy.
MICHAEL LEAPMAN

• • •

I'm passing the joints on Fourteenth Street between Third
and Fourth Avenues. I peeps under the swinging doors and
keeps thinking that the swellest job in the world is the guy
what bangs away on the piano. I wants to be him.
JIMMY DURANTE

• • •

The food was good cafe fodder and cheap and, at 2 AM,
helped to sober one up. Bill de Kooning usually stood at the
bar. . . . Jackson Pollock, by then living in the Hamptons,
might drop in while in New York. The tale is told that, one
night, he tore the door off the men's room. . . .
BENNETT SCHIFF, ON THE CEDAR STREET TAVERN IN
GREENWICH VILLAGE

• • •

Once one gets off the main commercial streets, one finds that the 19th-century city is surprisingly intact and, in parts, is unusually handsome. . . .
L. J. DAVIS

• • •

Among those tangled irregular streets to the west of Washington Square, I caught occasionally, from the taxi, a glimpse, almost eighteenth-century, of a lamp-less, black-windowed street-end where the street-urchins, shrieking in the silence, were stacking up bonfires in the snow.
EDMUND WILSON, *I THOUGHT OF DAISY*

• • •

She likes taxis. She travels in buses and subways only when she is trying to stop smoking. New York, the capsized city, half-capsized, anyway, with the inhabitants hanging on, most of them still able to laugh as they cling to their island that is their life's predicament.
MAEVE BRENNAN, *THE LONG-WINDED LADY: NOTES FROM THE NEW YORKER*

• • •

Evening is coming fast, and the great city is blazing there in your vision in its terrific frontal sweep and curtain of star-flung towers, now sown with the diamond pollen of a million lights, and the sun has set behind them, and the red light of fading day is painted upon the river.
THOMAS WOLFE

• • •

Ownerless pigs with battle-scarred ears amble about—and there are plenty of them here.
HENRYK SIENKIEWICZ, NOBEL PRIZE-WINNING
NOVELIST, WHILE VISITING
THE CITY IN 1876

• • •

New York is the concentrate of art and commerce and sport and religion and entertainment and finance, bringing to a single compact area the gladiator, the evangelist, the promoter, the actor, the trader and the merchant.
E. B. WHITE, *HERE IS NEW YORK*

• • •

The sun was low over the brownstones on the other side of the yard, and an ailanthus stood silhouetted against its golden rim, its budding branches forming a lace curtain through which a wind moved softly.
CHAIM POTOK, *THE CHOSEN*

• • •

High on the roof of one of the skyscrapers was a tin brass goat looking . . . out across silver snakes of winding rivers.
CARL SANDBURG, *ROOTABAGA STORIES*

• • •

The city stretches from dollhouse rows at the base of the park through a broad blurred bell of flowerpot red patched with tar roofs and twinkling cars.
JOHN UPDIKE, *RABBIT, RUN*

• • •

Follow that couple carrying a bag of ice.
A COMMON WAY, IN SOHO, TO FIND
AND CRASH A PARTY

• • •

The street where I now live has a quietness and sense of permanence that seem to belong to the nineteenth century. The street is very short. At one end, there are comfortable old houses, with gracious facades and pleasant back-yards in the rear.
CARSON MCCULLERS, "BROOKLYN IS MY NEIGHBORHOOD," *VOGUE,* 1941

• • •

I have the illusion of having put down roots here. I have spoken in most of the synagogues. They know me in some of the stores. Even the pigeons know me; the moment I come out with a bag of feed, they begin to fly toward me from blocks away.
ISAAC BASHEVIS SINGER, *A FRIEND OF KAFKA AND OTHER STORIES*

• • •

New York lay stretched in midsummer languor under her trees in her thinnest dress, idly and beautifully to the eyes of her lover.
E. B. WHITE, *POEMS AND SKETCHES OF E. B. WHITE*

• • •

It was one of those rainy late afternoons when the toy department of Woolworth's on Fifth Avenue is full of women who appear to have been taken in adultery and who are now shopping for a present to carry home to their youngest child.
JOHN CHEEVER

• • •

Mrs. O'Grady and the colonel's lady [are] close if uncommunicative neighbors. Here drying winter flannels are within fishpole reach of a Wall Street tycoon's windows, and the society woman in her boudoir may be separated only by a wall from the family on relief in a cold-water flat.
LOU CODY

• • •

At eighteen dollars a month, [our new apartment] was equipped with all sorts of conveniences that we Europeans were quite unused to: electric lights, gas cooking-range, bath, telephone, automatic service-elevator, and even a chute for the garbage. These things completely won the boys over to New York.
LEON TROTSKY, *MY LIFE,* 1930

• • •

The steaming clothes strung across the tenement kitchens;
bathing the newest baby; the apartments without air,
without light—there was never any ugliness or sordidness in
all this for me.
FANNY BRICE

• • •

A tenement canyon hung with fire-escapes, bed-clothing,
and faces. Always these faces at the tenement windows. The
street never failed them. It was an immense excitement. It
never slept. It roared like a sea. It exploded like fireworks.
MICHAEL GOLD, *JEWS WITHOUT MONEY*

• • •

When my parents moved to a more respectable and duller
part of the city, it held no interest whatever for me. I hired a
room in Hester Street in a wooden, ramshackle building that
seemed to date back at least a hundred years and, from my
window overlooking the market, made drawings daily.
JACOB EPSTEIN, *LET THERE BE SCULPTURE*

• • •

Any wall, any stoop, any curving metal edge on a billboard sign made a place against which to knock a ball; any bottom rung of a fire escape ladder a goal in basketball; any sewer cover a base; any crack in the pavement a "net" for the tense sharp tennis that we played . . .
ALFRED KAZIN, *A WALKER IN THE CITY*

• • •

The more gregarious arrange villages of their sections of the city, cultivating laconic chumminess in a local saloon or restaurant. The corner tailor freely offers his troubled autobiography after the second visit and the woman in the fish store is eager to teach Genoese tricks of fish cookery.
KATE SIMON

• • •

Mass is said in twenty-three different languages in this city.
ED KOCH, MAYOR, 1978–1989

• • •

A map of the city, colored to designate nationalities, would show more stripes than on the skin of a zebra, and more colors than a rainbow.
JACOB RIIS, *HOW THE OTHER HALF LIVES*

• • •

It is often said that New York is a city for only the very rich and the very poor. It is less often said that New York is also, at least for those of us who came there from somewhere else, a city for only the very young.
JOAN DIDION

• • •

Give me your tired, your poor, your huddled masses yearning to breathe free.
EMMA LAZARUS

• • •

The J train would with a certain wheezing ease through Queens and into Brooklyn. Birds could be heard, through the rumble, and graveyards and unopened schools flashed by outside the windows.
JOE SEXTON

• • •

Ride the New York subways one day. You could fall in love
or get snake bitten or see a baby born. Hear a conductor
do Elvis routines between stops. Buy a cabbage or a
condom. . . . Every car on the local trains that leave the
station will be filled to its "crush load" capacity of ISO–and
then, the records show, another 3.42 will pry themselves in.
JIM DWYER

• • •

Not everybody on the subway is demented. On the trains
that call at Wall Street you will see businessmen and women,
their clothes crumpled in the crush and heat, trying bravely
to read the *Wall Street Journal* by folding it
neatly in quarters.
MICHAEL LEAPMAN

• • •

Greater drama resides in the endless flow of activity that crowds the cars and platforms. Beggars, singers, banjo-players, and candy-butchers vie for a few pennies, howl bargains, or stumble silently past the apathetic passengers. Occasionally, a particularly bright singing troupe or an unusually pathetic cripple will meet with warm response.
LOU CODY

• • •

The city is itself a huge market. You can't go more than a few steps without finding a store of some sort. We are all potential entrepreneurs, looking to make a deal in this country of commerce.
JEROME CHARYN, *METROPOLIS*

• • •

Not to have seen those hucksters and their carts, and their merchandise, and their extraordinary zest for bargaining is to have missed a sight that once seen declines to be forgotten.
HARPER'S WEEKLY

• • •

Every detail matters. It is important to perceive that hardware stores are often painted orange out front, and that the color of newspaper kiosks and shoe shine stands is green.
NATHAN SILVER

• • •

"I really want those Gucci shoes," the good-looking young man told two friends as they walked across Prince Street. But one of them, a woman, was distracted. Pulling out her Nikon, she clicked away at a line of clean white laundry flapping from a line between two nearby brick tenements.
ANEMONA HARTOCOLUS

• • •

I can see myself as a very old man in a terrific wheel chair. Only, I won't be photographing the tree outside my window, the way Steichen did. I'll be photographing other old people.
RICHARD AVEDON

• • •

These skyscrapers, who belong to a brotherhood of giants, help each other to rise, to prop each other up, to soar until all sense of perspective disappears. You try to count the stories one by one, then your weary gaze starts to climb in tens.
PAUL MORAND, *NEW YORK*

• • •

Every man seems to feel that he has got the duties for two lifetimes to accomplish in one, and so he rushes, rushes, rushes, and never has time to be companionable—never has any time at his disposal to fool away on matters which do not involve dollars and duty and business.
MARK TWAIN

• • •

He used to stage a ritual called 'Chasing Pigeons' . . . . [He would] charge madly into a flock of complacent pigeons, shouting and waving his arms. The pigeons would take to the air, but always come wheeling back, for no pigeon can resist his curiosity about an erratic human being.
ROGER BUTTERFIELD, ON THE STRANGE BEHAVIOR OF ACTOR ZERO MOSTEL

• • •

He blinked . . . and suddenly, he could see. He was crouching
in the middle of a large meadow fringed with trees. Beyond
the trees, wreathed in fog and mist, dozens of giant buildings
were thrusting toward a leaden sky. There was a sign at the
top of one of them: Essex House.
GEORGE CHESBRO, *BONE*

• • •

. . . set off with George Anthon and Johnny to explore the
Central Park, which will be a feature of the city within five
years and a lovely place in A.D. 1900, when its trees will have
acquired dignity and appreciable diameters.
GEORGE TEMPLETON STRONG, *THE DIARY OF
GEORGE TEMPLETON STRONG*

• • •

It has felt like 5:30 PM in the lobby of the Algonquin Hotel
for nearly 90 years now . . . chronic, romantic twilight.
STEPHEN DRUCKER

• • •

The night John died, there were so many people outside
the Dakota. They were singing and playing John's songs . .
. . Hearing his songs in the street was very difficult for me.
I was sitting alone in our bedroom, which was on the 72nd
Street side, and John was singing all night.
YOKO ONO

• • •

Cut off as I am, it is inevitable that I should sometimes
feel like a shadow walking in a shadowy world. When
this happens I ask to be taken to New York City. Always I
return home weary but I have the comforting certainty that
mankind is real and I myself am not a dream.
HELEN KELLER

• • •

In its stride, New York takes on one more interior city,
to shelter, this time, all governments, and to clear the
slum called war. New York is not a capital city—it is not
a national capital or a state capital. But it is by way of
becoming the capital of the world.
E. B. WHITE

• • •

Right now a lot of people are still choosing to go to Toronto
instead of shooting in New York City, something I haven't
done and something I hope I'll never have to do.
SPIKE LEE

• • •

"Brace for impact."
SULLENBERGER'S ANNOUNCEMENT TO THOSE
ABOARD THE FLIGHT, AS RECOUNTED BY MULTIPLE
PASSENGERS ON THE PLANE, *NEW YORK TIMES,*
JAN. 16, 2009

• • •

[He] did a masterful job of landing the plane in the river
and then making sure that everybody got out. He walked the
plane twice after everybody else was off and tried to verify
that there was nobody else onboard, and he . . . made sure
that there was nobody behind him.
NEW YORK CITY MAYOR MICHAEL BLOOMBERG,
AT A POST-CRASH PRESS CONFERENCE, LAUDING
SULLENBERGER'S PERFORMANCE, JAN. 15, 2009

• • •

For most visitors to Manhattan, both foreign and domestic, New York is the Shrine of the Good Time. This is only natural, for outsiders come to New York for the sole purpose of having a good time, and it is for their New York hosts to provide it. The visiting Englishman, or the visiting Californian, is convinced that New York is made up of millions of gay pixies, flittering about constantly in a sophisticated manner in search of a new thrill. "I don't see how you stand it," they often say to the native New Yorker who has been sitting up past his bedtime for a week in an attempt to tire his guest out.

ROBERT BENCHLEY

• • •

When New York banned smoking in restaurants, I stopped eating out. When they banned it in the workplace I quit working, and when they raised the price of cigarettes to seven dollars a pack, I gathered all my stuff and went to France.

DAVID SEDARIS

• • •

One of the glories of New York is its ethnic food, and only McDonald's and Burger King equalize us all.
JOHN CORRY

• • •

New York's Fulton Street is the Vatican City of fish markets.
DAVID MICHAELIS

• • •

New York is the only city in the world where you can get deliberately run down on the sidewalk by a pedestrian.
RUSSELL BAKER, REPORTED IN RAND LINDSLY'S QUOTATIONS

• • •

"Roaming the streets of New York, we encountered many examples of this delightful quality of New Yorkers, forever on their toes, violently, restlessly involving themselves in the slightest situation brought to their attention, always posing alternatives, always ready with an answer or an argument."
JESSICA MITFORD, *HONS AND REBELS*

• • •

"New Yorkers do not amble, do not meander, and do not hesitate. Nor do they pay much attention to the world around them. New Yorkers are that way of necessity. To preserve a modicum of sanity in a city of borderline lunacy, they learn to screen out Manhattan's nerve-racking sights and sounds."
JOSEPH R. GARBER, *RASCAL MONEY*

• • •

"New Yorkers are prone to boast of their superiority over the denizens of other cities, but it is a fact that the American metropolis is inferior in culture, intelligence and morals to almost any city in the world. It is the home of big men with little soul, big newspapers with little editors."
HENRY O. MORRIS, *WAITING FOR THE SIGNAL*

• • •

New York blazes like a magnificent jewel in its fit setting of sea, and earth, and stars."
THOMAS WOLFE, *THE WEB AND THE ROCK (VOICES OF THE SOUTH)*

• • •

The gateway of America, and the most dazzling expressing of
its lingering diversity, is still the city of New York.
JAN MORRIS, *COAST TO COAST: A JOURNEY ACROSS
1950S AMERICA* (TRAVELERS' TALES CLASSICS)

• • •

The skyscrapers seemed like tall gravestones. I wondered
why, if the United States was so rich, as surely it was, did its
biggest city look so grotesque? At that moment I sensed for
the first time that people in New York could not be as happy
as we used to think they were back home.
BERNARDO VEGA, *MEMOIRS OF BERNARDO VEGA: A
CONTRIBUTION TO THE HISTORY OF THE PUERTO
RICAN COMMUNITY IN NEW YORK*

• • •

New York is a hellhole. And you know how I feel
about hellholes!
HOMER SIMPSON, *THE SIMPSONS*

• • •

New York is a sucked orange.
RALPH WALDO EMERSON, *THE CONDUCT OF LIFE*

• • •

New York, a dreamscape of opportunity, often presented a
flimsy mirage. Large houses rose around a sudden fortune
then disappeared in half a decade, blown away like stage
props.
ELLEN HORAN, *31 BOND STREET*

• • •

In dress, habits, manners, provincialism, routine and
narrowness, he acquired that charming insolence, that
irritating completeness, that sophisticated crassness, that
overbalanced poise that make the Manhattan gentleman so
delightfully small in his greatness.
O. HENRY

• • •

In its extravagance, its luxury, its expensiveness, its general carelessness with money, New York is like a child that has not learned self-restraint but has its pockets well filled.
ROBERT SHACKLETON, *THE BOOK OF NEW YORK*

• • •

I have never walked down Fifth Avenue alone without thinking of money. I have never walked there with a companion without talking of it.
ANTHONY TROLLOPE, *NORTH AMERICA*

• • •

The place: New York City. The time: Now, 1962. And there's no time or place like it. If you've got a dream, this is the place to make that dream come true. That's why the soaring population of hopeful dreamers has just reached eight million people. Oh! Make that eight million and one.
NARRATOR, *DOWN WITH LOVE*

• • •

That's the great thing about New York. You walk down the street and you encounter like a thousand potential sexual partners every day. A walk to the deli can be very erotic.
TOMMY (EDWARD BURNS), *SIDEWALKS OF NEW YORK*

• • •

This city here is like an open sewer, ya know; it's full of filth
and scum.
TRAVIS BICKLE (ROBERT DE NIRO), *TAXI DRIVER*

• • •

This is New York, Skyscraper Champion of the World . . .
Where the Slickers and Know-It-Alls peddle gold bricks to
each other . . . And where Truth, crushed to earth, rises again
more phony than a glass eye.
BEN HECHT, *NOTHING SACRED*

• • •

The thing that impressed me then as now about New
York . . . was the sharp, and at the same time immense,
contrast it showed between the dull and the shrewd, the
strong and the weak, the rich and the poor, the wise and the
ignorant . . . the strong, or those who ultimately dominated,
were so very strong, and the weak so very, very weak—
and so very, very many.
THEODORE DREISER

• • •

When you leave New York, you are astonished at how clean
the rest of the world is. Clean is not enough.
FRAN LEBOWITZ

• • •

"Been in the city long?" inquired the New Yorker, getting
ready for the exact tip against the waiter's coming with large
change from the bill. "Me?" said the man from Topaz City.
"Four days. Never in Topaz City, was you?" "I" said the New
Yorker. "I was never farther west than Eighth Avenue. I had
a brother who died on Ninth, but I met the cortege at Eighth
. . . I cannot say I am familiar with the West."
O. HENRY

• • •

One day there was four innocent people shot. That's the
best shooting done in this town. Hard to find four innocent
people in New York.
WILL ROGERS

• • •

As we drew near New York I was at first amused, and then somewhat staggered, by the cautious and grisly tales that went around. You would have thought we were to land upon a cannibal island. You must speak to no one in the streets, as they would not leave 'til you were rooked and beaten. You must enter a hotel lobby with military precautions; for the least you had to apprehend was to awake the next morning without money and baggage, or necessary raiment, a lone forked radish in a bed; and if the worst befell, you would instantly and mysteriously disappear from the ranks of mankind.
ROBERT LEWIS STEVENSON

• • •

Skyscraper national park.
KURT VONNEGUT

• • •

New York makes one think of the collapse of civilization, about Sodom and Gomorrah, the end of the world. The end wouldn't come as a surprise here. Many people already bank on it.
SAUL BELLOW

PART FOUR

• • •

What Do New Yorkers Talk about When They Talk about Themselves?

My dream was to have a Library of Congress catalogue number, that's all.
FRANK MCCOURT, ON THE PUBLICATION OF
ANGELA'S ASHES, HIS FIRST BOOK

• • •

I don't mind being called Meathead.
ROB REINER, ON HIS LIFE AS ARCHIE BUNKER'S SON-IN-LAW

• • •

I'm sick to death of being a one-dimensional character.
I'm just a guy in a tight suit and a snap-brim hat. I have no
function except to carry the plot and get killed in the end to
prove that virtue is triumphant.
HUMPHREY BOGART

• • •

I have to be a little bit in love with my models.
RICHARD AVEDON

• • •

When I go on the talk shows, I project what I am—an
intelligent and well-educated girl from Brooklyn.
BEVERLY SILLS

• • •

I knew I had talent and I was afraid that if I learned to type I would become a secretary.
BARBRA STREISAND

• • •

No one seemed to care what I was doing so long as the record showed I had finished a full day's work. Therefore after lunchtime I kept my head bent low while I was writing short stories at my desk.
BERNARD MALAMUD, ON HIS CAREER STRATEGY AS A CLERK AT THE CENSUS BUREAU

• • •

I quit my job just to quit. I didn't quit my job to write fiction. I just didn't want to work anymore.
DON DELILLO

• • •

I think I've made a difference in my phase of the broadcast industry, but I don't think I've impacted on the world in the manner of Franklin Roosevelt.
HOWARD COSELL

• • •

Gore Vidal isn't what I set out to be. Early on I wanted to be
Franklin Roosevelt.
GORE VIDAL

• • •

Not since *David Copperfield* have I read such a stirring and
inspiring life story.
GROUCHO MARX, "REVIEWING" HIS OWN
AUTOBIOGRAPHY

• • •

Once a song-and-dance man, always a song-and-dance man.
Those few words tell as much about me professionally as
there is to tell.
JIMMY CAGNEY

• • •

I always wanted to be some kind of writer or newspaper
reporter. But after college—I did other things.
JACQUELINE KENNEDY ONASSIS

• • •

That was always my experience—a poor boy in a rich town; a poor boy in a rich boy's school; a poor boy in a rich man's club at Princeton . . . I have never been able to forgive the rich for being rich, and it has colored my entire life and works.
F. SCOTT FITZGERALD, IN A LETTER TO HIS
AGENT'S WIFE

• • •

My father was the editor of an agricultural magazine called the *Southern Planter.* He didn't think of himself as a writer. He was a scientist, an agronomist, but I thought of him as a writer because I'd seen him working at his desk. . . . I just assumed that I was going to do that.
TOM WOLFE

• • •

So I started writing poetry when I was six. . . . When I was fifteen I wrote seven hundred pages of an incredibly bad novel—it's a very funny book I still like a lot.
EDWARD ALBEE

• • •

I assumed when writing it [Howl] that it was something that *could* not be published because I wouldn't want my daddy to see what was in there. About my sex life . . .
ALLEN GINSBERG

• • •

Very often I'll feel a certain shame for what I've done with a novel. I won't say it's the novel that's bad; I'll say it's I who was bad. Almost as if the novel did not really belong to me, as if it was something raised by me like a child.
NORMAN MAILER

• • •

When I'm finished with a piece, I'm embarrassed to look at it again, as I though I were afraid I hadn't wiped its nose clean.
J. D. SALINGER, IN A LETTER TO A FRIEND

• • •

I'm a simple guy. For a comedian, I'm surprisingly normal. I have never been to a psychiatrist and I've only been married once.
JACK BENNY

• • •

When I'm close to finishing a book, nothing is more important to me. I might stop to save a life, but nothing less.
JOSEPH HELLER

• • •

If I'm going to be remembered as a novelist, I'd better produce a few more books.
RALPH ELLISON

• • •

When the lyrics are right, it's easier for me to write a tune than to bend over and tie my shoelaces.
RICHARD RODGERS

• • •

What Do New Yorkers Talk about When They Talk about Themselves?

Of all my parents' friends, the only one happy going to work was a member of 120 Truck. I was only 16 then, but that is when I decided I wanted to be a fireman.
PETER J. GANCI JR., CHIEF OF DEPARTMENT, FDNY

• • •

I was about thirty-eight at the time, and thought I ought to get into abstractions, whatever they are. This attitude bewildered the instructors at several Paris art schools . . . . My best efforts were some modernistic things that looked like very lousy Matisses.
NORMAN ROCKWELL

• • •

I'd like to make a great film. I haven't made one yet. You don't start out to make a great film, you start out to make the idea you have at the time. But . . . maybe I'll get lucky and one or two will turn out to be terrific films.
WOODY ALLEN

• • •

I was brought up to be the . . . fat, happy child who would marry someone in the Racquet Club and drive around in a station wagon to pick up the twelve children and bring them home to the rose-covered cottage. Now I'm just the opposite, and I'm glad.
LEE RADZIWILL

• • •

I wanted a perfect ending. Now I've learned, the hard way, that some poems don't rhyme, and some stories don't have a clear beginning, middle, and end. Life is about not knowing, having to change, taking the moment and making the best of it.
GILDA RADNER

• • •

That whole show was completely beyond me. I never understood what was going on. They'd tell me to go over there and trip, so I'd go over there and trip.
BOB KEESHAN, AKA CAPTAIN KANGAROO, ON HIS EARLY WORK ON *THE HOWDY DOODY SHOW* AS CLARABELL THE CLOWN

• • •

It's my dream to be a member of the Rat Pack. I never thought about being a sitcom star. I thought about being Sammy Davis Jr.
TONY DANZA

• • •

I knew I was going to be a comedian at a very young age. I remember one time I made a friend laugh so hard he sprayed a mouthful of cookies and milk all over me, and I liked it.
JERRY SEINFELD

• • •

In kindergarten I flunked sandpile.
JOEY BISHOP

• • •

Carmela can cook, but God knows I can't.
EDIE FALCO, AKA CARMELA SOPRANO

• • •

I couldn't tell a joke if you put a gun to my head.
NEIL SIMON

• • •

I'm very proud of my Irish side also . . . I went there when
I broke up with my girlfriend . . . [but] all you do is drink
Guinness and cry and look at the ocean and want to kill
yourself.
BEN STILLER

• • •

I never heard Archie's kind of talk in my own family. Mine
was a family of teachers . . . . My father was a lawyer and
was in partnership with two Jews . . . . There were two black
families in our circle of friends. My father disliked talk like
Archie's—he called it the hallmark of ignorance.
CARROLL O'CONNOR

• • •

If you live in New York, even if you're Catholic,
you're Jewish.
LENNY BRUCE

• • •

I have no hobbies, no recreations. I hate sports. I also hate gardening and walking. I don't go to movies or the theatre or watch television. What I do like is lying down. My best thinking is done going into or coming out of naps.
JOSEPH HELLER

• • •

My first recorded success was at five years of age when I drew a cow with all her equipment. At eight I drew palm trees which I remember as being very fine. Fortunately, none has survived.
MARGARET AYER

• • •

The family had gone for a ride in the subway and when we came home I drew a picture of the conductor. The shape of his cap fascinated me. Anyway, my mother said, Sydney is an artist, and I've been trying to live up to her words ever since.
SYDNEY HOFF

• • •

We were smothered with opportunity—piano lessons, skating lessons, summer camps, art school. For a long time I wanted to be a painter. But there were so many painters in the family, and poetry was something nobody else did.
ERICA JONG

• • •

What Do New Yorkers Talk about When They Talk about Themselves?

I touched it. It made pretty sounds. Right away I screamed,
"Ma, give me lessons."
LEONARD BERNSTEIN, ON THE MOMENT HE FIRST
TOOK INTEREST IN MUSIC

• • •

When I was a child, until the age of thirteen, I wanted
passionately to be a chemist.
SUSAN SONTAG

• • •

He said it was because I loved horses, but I think he had this
dream that I'd lose my accent.
PENNY MARSHALL, ON WHY HER FATHER SENT HER
TO COLLEGE AT THE UNIVERSITY OF NEW MEXICO

• • •

I have an overly protective mother, and I never went out of
my neighborhood until I became legal age. And then I just
went over to the West Side, planted my foot down so I could
say that I had been there, and ran right back home.
CHRIS ELLIOTT

• • •

One weird experience with matrimony made me respect the institution. I knew that I had broken a promise, a bargain, a contract. If I were to get into the habit of doing that, my word would not be worth the breath that spoke it in any other agreement.
MAE WEST, *GOODNESS HAD NOTHING TO DO WITH IT*

• • •

Women, horses, cars, clothes. I did it all. And do you know what that's called? It's called "living."
CAB CALLOWAY

• • •

I divide women into two categories. The female and the broad. Me? I'm a broad.
BETTE DAVIS

• • •

Every morning it takes me hours to get ready. The first time I saw myself naked in a school locker room, I was like, "Wow." After that, everything had to be trimmed, oiled and together.
CUBA GOODING JR.

• • •

I can't wait until tomorrow . . . because I get better looking
every day.
JOE NAMATH

• • •

There's a million good-looking guys, but I'm a novelty.
JIMMY DURANTE

• • •

Well, I get on the bus; I put on my makeup; I study my
notes; I read the paper. It's really—I'm really taking the bus
because I'm cheap.
HELEN GURLEY BROWN, *MANHATTAN PASSIONS*

• • •

People are afraid to hug me because they know I'm not a
huggy guy.
RAY ROMANO

• • •

I wound up putting a big sign on the front lawn listing all the people I didn't like. The list included the whole block, and I moved away amidst cheers and lawsuits.
JIMMY BRESLIN

• • •

If you pet me, I'll purr. But if you hit me, I might scratch.
LEONA HELMSLEY

• • •

I think I'm still an Impressionist.
EDWARD HOPPER

• • •

Don't you see the rest of the country looks upon New York like we're left-wing, communist, Jewish, homosexual pornographers? I think of us that way sometimes and I live here.
ALVY SINGER, *ANNIE HALL*

• • •

I miss New York. I still love how people talk to you on the
street—just assault you and tell you what they think
of your jacket.
MADONNA

• • •

I live in New York City, the stories of my films take place in
New York; I'm a New York filmmaker.
SPIKE LEE

• • •

I don't like Los Angeles. The people are
awful and terribly shallow, and everybody wants to
be famous but nobody wants to play the game. I'm from
New York. I will kill to get what I need.
LADY GAGA

• • •

No place epitomizes the American experience and the
American spirit more than New York City.
MICHAEL BLOOMBERG

• • •

New York, concrete jungle where dreams are made, oh there's nothing you can't do. Now you're in New York, these streets will make you feel brand new, big lights will inspire you. Let's hear it for New York.
"EMPIRE STATE OF MIND"—JAY-Z FT. ALICIA KEYS

• • •

New York, I love you but you're bringing me down.
LCD SOUNDSYSTEM

• • •

If you walk the sidewalks in the Big Apple, you should always walk closer to the buildings. The sidewalks curve a little, and that way you seem to be much taller.
DUSTIN HOFFMAN

• • •

This is the town that never sleeps. That's why we don't live in Duluth. That plus I don't know where Duluth is.
WOODY ALLEN

• • •

What Do New Yorkers Talk about When They Talk about Themselves?

My name is Lady Gaga, and I was born and raised in the unbreakable streets of New York City. Thank you so much. Tonight, I want you to forget all of your insecurities because I didn't used to be brave but you have made me brave, Little Monsters.
LADY GAGA AT A CONCERT IN NEW YORK CITY /
FEBRUARY 22, 2011

• • •

Eight million stories out there, and they're naked. City is a pity, half of y'all won't make it.
"EMPIRE STATE OF MIND"—JAY-Z FT. ALICIA KEYS

• • •

Even the vegetables in New York are better. It's not just the vegetables, of course. I look out the window and I see the lights and the skyline and the people on the street rushing around looking for action, love, and the world's greatest chocolate chip cookie, and my heart does a little dance.
NORA EPHRON, *HEARTBURN*

• • •

I can't with any conscience argue for New York with anyone. It's like Calcutta. But I love the city in an emotional, irrational way, like loving your mother or your father even though they're a drunk or a thief. I've loved the city my whole life—to me, it's like a great woman.
WOODY ALLEN, *WOODY ALLEN: INTERVIEWS*
(CONVERSATIONS WITH FILMMAKERS SERIES)

• • •

I have dreamt a lifetime to get on this flight to New York. I don't care if it's summer. Leather, high heels, and a bad attitude. Here I come.
LADY GAGA

• • •

New York, you got money on your mind and my words won't make a dime's worth a difference. So here's to you New York.
SIMON AND GARFUNKEL, "A HEART IN NEW YORK"

• • •

Manhattan is an accumulation of possible disasters that never happen.
REM KOOLHAAS

• • •

PART FIVE

New York City Wisdom

Everybody credits me as saying that kissing Marilyn was like
kissing Hitler. I never said that. I did more than kiss her . . .
But we knew it was never going to work out between us, you
know, rubbing and kissing doesn't always mean you're going
to fall madly in love.
TONY CURTIS

• • •

Hollywood's a place where they'll pay you a thousand dollars for a kiss, and fifty cents for your soul. I know, because I turned down the first offer often enough and held out for the fifty cents.
MARILYN MONROE, *MARILYN MONROE IN HER OWN WORDS*

• • •

It's hard to convince a girl's parents that a revolutionary fugitive with a vasectomy is a good deal.
ABBIE HOFFMAN

• • •

Elephants are no harder to teach than ballerinas.
GEORGE BALANCHINE, ON HIS WORK DIRECTING RINGLING BROTHERS' ELEPHANTS IN A BALLET

• • •

If you want to live a long time you have to smoke cigars, drink martinis and dance close.
GEORGE BURNS

• • •

You got to be careful if you don't know where you're going, because you might not get there.
YOGI BERRA

• • •

To get as old as I am [91] one must drink a glass of whiskey every morning, smoke a long cigar and chase beautiful girls.
ARTHUR RUBINSTEIN

• • •

I've never had a hangover. I think it's because I don't smoke.
BERNARD "TOOTS" SHOR

• • •

Some of us are becoming the men we wanted to marry.
GLORIA STEINEM

• • •

If people would just take my advice, everything would go well.
WILLIAM F. BUCKLEY JR.

• • •

I have been poor and I have been rich. Rich is better.
SOPHIE TUCKER

• • •

Money isn't everything as long as you have enough.
MALCOLM FORBES

• • •

If I knew 1'd live this long, I would have taken better
care of myself.
MICKEY MANTLE

• • •

All I know about getting out a magazine is to print what you
think is good (or as near to your standard as you can get)
and let nature take its course: if enough readers think as you
do, you're a success, if not you're a failure.
HAROLD ROSS, FOUNDER AND EDITOR OF THE *NEW
YORKER*

• • •

I write on the right and I keep notes on the left, ideas that come, and then I pick them up later on. Then I go and sit at the keyboard and type it in and refine. So the pen for me is mightier than the word processor.

FRANK MCCOURT

• • •

The idea is to get the pencil moving quickly. I go over and over a page. Either it bleeds and shows its beginnings to be human, or the form emits shadows of itself and I'm off. I have a terrible will that way.

BERNARD MALAMUD

• • •

Just as Faulkner came from the South, I came from Jewish Orthodox. And writers who write seriously, write about what they know best.

CHAIM POTOK

• • •

I don't think any pregnant woman should read it, but the obstetrician did read it and loved it.

IRA LEVIN, AUTHOR OF *ROSEMARY'S BABY,* ON WHY HE WOULDN'T LET HIS OWN WIFE READ THE BOOK

• • •

A writer in New York is a little bit like a tree falling in a forest. You're never sure if somebody's going to hear you.
LUCINDA FRANKS

• • •

A rising tide raises all ships.
ANONYMOUS WALL STREET ADAGE

• • •

The worst part of having success is to try to find someone who is happy for you.
BETTE MIDLER

• • •

There may be said to be two classes of people in the world: those who constantly divide the people of the world into two classes and those who do not.
ROBERT BENCHLEY

• • •

I know that it is no longer the fashion to emphasize subject in fiction, but the more I read, the more I think it matters.
LOUIS AUCHINCLOSS

• • •

New York City Wisdom

If you stay with newspaper work, you hit a point of no return, your talent levels out and diminishes, and . . . you retire without even knowing it.
DAVID HALBERSTAM

• • •

You start with the philosophy that theater is important to people's lives. If you don't believe this, then you might as well give up.
JOE PAPP

• • •

Art is what you can get away with.
ANDY WARHOL

• • •

Everybody can act, because everybody lies.
GEORGE ABBOTT

• • •

Televiso ergo sum-I am televised, therefore I am.
RUSSELL BAKER

• • •

No New Yorker should take Rupert Murdoch's *New York Post* seriously any longer. It makes *Hustler* magazine look like the Harvard Law Review.
ABE BEAME, MAYOR, 1974–1977

• • •

The singin's easy. Memorizing the words is hard.
ROCKY GRAZIANO, ON HIS NYC NIGHTCLUB DEBUT

• • •

If I had to give young writers advice, I would say, don't listen
to writers talking about writing or about themselves.
LILLIAN HELLMAN

• • •

A good many young writers make the mistake of enclosing
a stamped, self-addressed envelope, big enough for
the manuscript to come back in. This is too much of a
temptation to the editor.
RING LARDNER, *HOW TO WRITE SHORT STORIES,* 1954

• • •

Red keeps you awake, don't you think?
MARY HIGGINS CLARK, ON HER CHOICE OF COLOR
FOR THE WALLS IN HER OFFICE

• • •

A screenplay is a piece of carpentry, and except in the case of
Ingmar Bergman, it's not an art, it's a craft. And you want to
be as good as you can at your craft.
WILLIAM GOLDMAN

• • •

Taking pictures is like tiptoeing into the kitchen late at night
and stealing Oreo cookies.
DIANE ARBUS

• • •

I was drawing little Mickey Mouses for my children, working
from bubble-gum wrappers. I thought I'd do one of the
comics as is, large, just to see what it would look like.
ROY LICHTENSTEIN, ON THE BIRTH OF POP ART

• • •

I began life with the assumption that half the painters in the
world were women.
ELAINE DE KOONING

• • •

I have friends who see themselves as the public sees them,
and they are stone.
MIKE NICHOLS

• • •

I've come to realize that a big part of life is to smile when
you turn in at night.
KAREEM ABDUL–JABBAR

• • •

There is no question that there is an unseen world. The
problem is, how far is it from midtown and how late
is it open?
WOODY ALLEN

• • •

They say life's what happens when you're busy making other
plans. But sometimes in New York, life is what happens
when you're waiting for a table.
CARRIE BRADSHAW, *SEX AND THE CITY*

• • •

Everybody in New York City knows there's way more cars than parking spaces. You see cars driving in New York all hours of the night. It's like musical chairs except everybody sat down around 1964.
JERRY SEINFELD

• • •

I moved to New York City for my health. I'm paranoid and it was the only place where my fears were justified.
ANITA WEISS

• • •

In New York it's not whether you win or lose—it's how you lay the blame.
FRAN LEBOWITZ

• • •

Manhattan is a narrow island off the coast of New Jersey devoted to the pursuit of lunch.
RAYMOND SOKOLOV

• • •

In Washington, the first thing people tell you is what their job is. In Los Angeles you learn their star sign. In Houston you're told how rich they are. And in New York they tell you what their rent is.
SIMON HOGGART

• • •

Every true New Yorker believes with all his heart that when a New Yorker is tired of New York, he is tired of life.
ROBERT MOSES

• • •

This city is an addiction.
TIMOTHY LEARY

• • •

The gay straight man was a new strain of heterosexual male spawned in Manhattan as the result of overexposure to fashion, exotic cuisine, musical theatre and antique furniture.
CARRIE BRADSHAW, *SEX AND THE CITY*

• • •

A New Yorker who does not take the subway is not a New Yorker you can trust.
MOZZIE, *WHITE COLLAR*

• • •

The most irritating thing of all is that New Yorkers really don't care what you say about their city.
RUSSELL BAKER

• • •

How many New Yorkers does it take to screw in a lightbulb? None of your fucking business.
LYNNE TILLMAN, *NO LEASE ON LIFE*

• • •

In New York people check each other out to find out who they are, whereas in other cities there's no reason to bother since no one is ever anyone. As Stan used to say, "Half the people in New York if they were anywhere else would be either interviewed or arrested."
EDMUND WHITE, *CITY BOY*

• • •

For generations —since long before the great cities of this country became associated in the public mind with their problems rather than their wonders— New Yorkers have believed in the old saying that they learn at their mother's knee: "If you can't say something nice, you're never in danger of being taken for an out-of-towner."
CALVIN TRILLIN, "WHAT'S THE GOOD WORD?" *THE SUBWAY CHRONICLES*

• • •

Better a square foot of New York than all the rest of the world in a lump—better a lamppost on Broadway than the brightest star in the sky.
TEXAS GUINAN, *TEXAS GUINAN: QUEEN OF THE NIGHT CLUBS*

• • •

In New York, boy, money really talks—I'm not kidding.
J. D. SALINGER, *THE CATCHER IN THE RYE*

• • •

It's a law of New York City: no matter how much money you're making, you're surrounded by people making more.
BRIDIE CLARK, *THE OVERNIGHT SOCIALITE*

• • •

If you are going to live in New York it is well first to take the precaution of being a millionaire.
GEORGE WARRINGTON STEEVENS, *THE LAND OF THE DOLLAR*

• • •

Being miserable and treating other people like dirt is every New Yorker's God-given right.
THE MAYOR, *GHOSTBUSTERS 2*

• • •

There are certain sections of New York, Major, that I wouldn't advise you to try to invade.
RICK BLAINE, *CASABLANCA*

• • •

I'm gonna audition for a Broadway play, because if I can't make it there, I can't make it anyplace.
JACK MCFARLAND, *WILL & GRACE*

• • •

Every year the women of New York leave the past behind and look forward to the future . . . this is known as Fashion Week.
CARRIE BRADSHAW, *SEX AND THE CITY: THE MOVIE*

• • •

It would be a great exercise for someone who thinks they want to move to New York. Sit in an enclosed space full of fumes and hold hands with a stranger for twenty minutes while everyone around you speaks a language you don't understand. If you enjoy this, you will enjoy the 6 train.
TINA FEY, *BOSSYPANTS*

• • •

You know what I like about Manhattan? No mosquitoes.
FRANK COSTANZA, *SEINFELD*

• • •

It wasn't until I got to New York that I became Kansan. Everyone there kept reminding me they were Jewish or Irish, or whatever, so I kept reminding them that I was Midwestern. Before I knew it, I actually began to brag about being from Kansas! I discovered I had something a bit unique, but it was the nature of New York that forced me to claim my past.
WILLIAM INGE

• • •

Not only is New York the nation's melting pot, it is also the casserole, the chafing dish and the charcoal grill
MAYOR JOHN V. LINDSAY

• • •

The city is not a concrete jungle, it is a human zoo.
DESMOND MORRIS

• • •

Most human beings are driven to seek security and comfort. But there is another group that can only thrive on change and the unexpected of New York.
CATHLEEN NESBITT

• • •

I've been in New York for ten years, and the only people who are nice to us turn out to be Moonies.
P. J. O'ROURKE

PART SIX

• • •

Spoken Like a True New Yorker

Truman could not tell you the truth about anything. He was
a psychopath, and the lies would get crazier and crazier.
GORE VIDAL, ON TRUMAN CAPOTE

• • •

He is a sphinx without a secret.
TRUMAN CAPOTE, ON ANDY WARHOL

• • •

He decocts matters of the first philosophical magnitude from an examination of his own ordure, and I am not talking about his books.
WILLIAM F. BUCKLEY, ON NORMAN MAILER

• • •

It is one of the sublime provincialities of New York that its inhabitants lap up trivial gossip about essential nobodies they've never set eyes on, while continuing to boast that they could live elsewhere for twenty years without so much as exchanging pleasantries with their neighbors across the hall.
LOUIS KRONENBERGER, *COMPANY MANNERS,* 1954

• • •

It's difficult to get terribly interested in food I digested forty-five years ago.
DOROTHY PARKER, ON WHAT SHE AND HER FAMOUS WRITER FRIENDS ATE AT THEIR REGULAR HAUNT—THE ALGONQUIN ROUND TABLE AT THE ALGONQUIN HOTEL

• • •

A newspaper reported I spend *$30,000* a year buying Paris clothes and that women hate me for it. I couldn't spend that much unless I wore sable underwear.
JACQUELINE KENNEDY ONASSIS

• • •

[New Yorkers are] people who get acquainted with their neighbors by meeting them in Miami.
MARJORIE STEELE

• • •

[Like] most native New Yorkers I was born out of town . . . .
HARRY HERSHFIELD, AKA MR. NEW YORK

• • •

I was aware that I didn't know anything about making films, but I believed I couldn't make them any worse than the majority of films I was seeing. Bad films gave me the courage to try making a movie.
STANLEY KUBRICK

• • •

My movies cost less than a director's salary on [an average film]. When you work as cheap as I do, the studio hands you the money and tells you to go off with your friends and have fun.
CHRIS GUEST

• • •

We wondered why all superheroes should be rich. Couldn't they be worried about money instead? The more we thought about these things, the more we enjoyed what we were doing.
STAN LEE, COMIC BOOK PUBLISHER

• • •

Success to me is having ten honeydew melons, and eating only the top half of each one.
BARBRA STREISAND

• • •

People seem to enjoy things more when they know a lot of other people have been left out of the pleasure.
RUSSELL BAKER

• • •

If Congress insists on making stupid mistakes and passing foolish tax laws, millionaires should not be condemned if they take advantage of them.
J. P. MORGAN

• • •

I may not look like a Senator, but I think I'm what a Senator should look like.
BELLA ABZUG

• • •

If you elect a matinee idol mayor, you're going to have a musical comedy administration.
ROBERT MOSES, ON NYC MAYOR JOHN V. LINDSAY

• • •

What do I care about the law? Hain't I got the power?
CORNELIUS VANDERBILT

• • •

I'm not the type to get ulcers. I give them.
ED KOCH, MAYOR, 1978–1989

• • •

I could answer the question exactly the way you want, but if I did, I would hate myself in the morning.
RING LARDNER, TO THE HOUSE UN-AMERICAN ACTIVITIES COMMITTEE

• • •

I can't cut my conscience to fit this year's fashions.
LILLIAN HELLMAN, TO THE HOUSE UN-AMERICAN ACTIVITIES COMMITTEE

• • •

People romanticize it. These were no giants. Think of who was writing in those days–Lardner, Fitzgerald, Faulkner, and Hemingway. Those were the real giants. The round table was just a lot of people telling jokes and telling each other how good they were.
DOROTHY PARKER, ON THE ALGONQUIN ROUND TABLE

• • •

My relatives say they are glad I'm rich, but that they simply cannot read me.
KURT VONNEGUT

• • •

See that gold Cadillac down the street? That's the color I want those handrails. Gold. Cadillac gold. Not yellow like a daisy.
DONALD TRUMP, ON THE HANDRAILS IN TRUMP TOWER

• • •

Donald has never had the net worth he claimed. What he did have was trophy properties, brass balls, and a big mouth.
A LAWYER FRIEND OF THE DONALD'S

• • •

We ought to change the sign on the Statue of Liberty to read, "This time around, send us your rich."
FELIX ROHATYN

• • •

Real equality is going to come not when a female Einstein is recognized as quickly as a male Einstein, but when a female schlemiel is promoted as quickly as a male schlemiel.
BELLA ABZUG, ACCORDING TO MARLO THOMAS

• • •

I'm going to tell people Jackie left it to me. After she said goodbye to the kids, she said, "Give this to Joan."
JOAN RIVERS, ON JACKIE ONASSIS'S COSTUME JEWELRY AND, IN PARTICULAR, A GOLD AND BLACK-ENAMEL LIGHTER STAMPED WITH THE INITIAL J.

• • •

We should have a secret meeting in the cellar of the St. James Theatre, raise $25 million, put on a million-dollar failure and split it up.
MEL BROOKS, ON THE SUCCESS OF HIS HIT MUSICAL *THE PRODUCERS*

• • •

I'll live to see the day, Sir, when you have to earn a living by
going around Wall Street with a hand organ.
HENRY N. SMITH, FINANCIER

• • •

Maybe you will, Henry, maybe you will. And when I want a
monkey, Henry, I'll send for you.
JASON GOULD, SMITH'S FORMER PARTNER,
FINANCIER

• • •

Being an actor is like being a currency in the currency
exchange. Today they are going, "Hey, you're the Deutsche
mark. We think you're great. Wake up; it's not a dream."
Then they turn around the next day and say, "Hey, we
changed our minds. Somebody else is the Deutsche mark.
You're the peso."
ALEC BALDWIN

• • •

Twenty-five bucks a week; hours from eight in the evening
until unconscious.
JIMMY DURANTE, ON HIS JOB AT DIAMOND TONY'S
SALOON ON CONEY ISLAND

• • •

Even though I know I look like a football player wearing a
dress, in my mind's eye I'm beautiful.
HARVEY FIERSTEIN

• • •

In the '40s and '50s . . . men put on their dinner jackets.
Women wore evening gowns. I wore evening gowns.
MILTON BERLE

• • •

You know, I've actually had two children with the same
woman. That's certainly a sign of maturity, don't you think?
JAMES CAAN

• • •

Even Superman can't make a commitment. Why give me a hard time?
JERRY SEINFELD

• • •

I have considered it. That's why I'm single.
EVANGELINE BOOTH, GENERAL OF THE
INTERNATIONAL SALVATION ARMY, WHEN A FRIEND
SUGGESTED THAT SHE HAD REACHED AN AGE AT
WHICH SHE SHOULD CONSIDER GETTING MARRIED

• • •

You know how to whistle, don't you, Steve? You just put your lips together and . . . blow.
LAUREN BACALL, IN THE MOVIE *TO HAVE AND HAVE NOT*

• • •

It was love on the run with half the buttons undone.
MAE WEST, ON HER RELATIONSHIP WITH GEORGE RAFT

• • •

She told me to take off my pants. When I told her that I couldn't, because I didn't have any underwear on, she told me, "That's all right. If you had, I'd ask you to take it off too."
A BODYBUILDER AUDITIONING FOR MAE WEST

• • •

The city had beaten the pants off me. Whatever it required to get ahead, I didn't have. I didn't leave the city in disgust-I left it with the respect plain unadulterated fear gives.
JOHN STEINBECK, ON HIS FIRST STINT IN NEW YORK

• • •

Dancers are stripped enough onstage. You don't have to know more about them than they've given you already. I want to see people dance and I would like to guess what kind of people they are. I don't want to know the recipe for [their] pasta.
MIKHAIL BARYSHNIKOV

• • •

I dress for women—and I undress for men.
ANGIE DICKINSON

• • •

The world is an oyster, but you don't crack it open on a
mattress.
ARTHUR MILLER, *DEATH OF A SALESMAN*

• • •

I think I made his back feel better.
MARILYN MONROE, REFERRING TO HER
RELATIONSHIP WITH JFK

• • •

He was getting over a four-day drunk, and I was getting over
a four-year marriage.
LILLIAN HELLMAN, ON HER FIRST MEETING WITH
DASHIELL HAMMETT

• • •

A good saloonkeeper is the most important man in the
community.
BERNARD "TOOTS" SHOR

• • •

My first qualification for this great office is my monumental
personal ingratitude.
FIORELLO LA GUARDIA, TO JOB SEEKERS FOLLOWING
HIS ELECTION

• • •

One of the brightest people I know is Shirley MacLaine, and
Shirley is, of course, a firm believer in astrology. And in her
defense I'll say this—that I have known Shirley MacLaine
ever since she was a cocker spaniel and I . . .
STEVE ALLEN

• • •

She's gone to Bloomingdale's.
ANDY WARHOL, WHEN ASKED ABOUT HIS MOTHER'S
DEATH

• • •

I bet you, Ziggie, a hundred bucks that he ain't here.
ATTRIBUTED TO THEATER PRODUCER CHARLES
DILLINGHAM, WHISPERED TO FLORENZ ZIEGFIELD
AS THEY CARRIED HARRY HOUDINI'S CASKET AWAY
AS PALLBEARERS

• • •

New York people will never go into a hole in the ground to ride . . . preposterous!
RUSSELL SAGE, ON THE NEWS IN 1900 THAT A RAILROAD WILL BE BUILT BENEATH MANHATTAN

• • •

Meditation for most New Yorkers is thinking about their next apartment, the bigger one.
WILLIAM L. HAMILTON

• • •

In New York we simply assumed that we were the best—in baseball as well as intellect, in brashness and in subtlety, in everything—and it would have been unseemly to remark upon such an obvious fact.
MICHAEL HARRINGTON, *FRAGMENTS OF THE CENTURY*

• • •

Rolling Stone is not just about music, but also about the things and attitudes that music embraces. To describe it any further would be difficult without sounding like bullshit, and bullshit is like gathering moss.
JANN WENNER

• • •

It is true that I enjoyed my celebrity status in my previous position, but I can prove that when I left Washington I wore exactly the same size crown as when I arrived.
HENRY KISSINGER

• • •

Spoken Like a True New Yorker

Even in high school, I could write smoothly and well,
long before I had anything to say.
LAWRENCE BLOCK

• • •

I won't quit until I get run over by a truck, a producer or a
critic.
JACK LEMMON

• • •

When I go, I'll take New Year's Eve with me.
GUY LOMBARDO

• • •

I agree with the Bogart Theory that all an actor owes the
public is a good performance.
LAUREN BACALL

• • •

If you don't like my identity, you won't like the magazine.
TINA BROWN, ON *VANITY FAIR*

• • •

Neither has anyone else.
JOSEPH HELLER, ON COMPLAINTS THAT HE NEVER
WROTE ANOTHER BOOK LIKE *CATCH-22*

• • •

A great many people have come up to me and asked me how I manage to get so much work done and still keep looking so dissipated. My answer is "Don't you wish you knew?"
ROBERT BENCHLEY, *HOW TO GET THINGS DONE*

• • •

I write out of outrage. My neighborhood, for example, pisses me off, with the drugs, crime, and homelessness. But I'm afraid of what happens the day I wake up and find I'm no longer angry about anything.
CALEB CARR

• • •

Freud's stupid. I didn't like Jung or Adler either. I go along with Samuel Goldwyn: he said anybody who has to see a psychiatrist ought to have to have his head examined.
MICKEY SPILLANE

• • •

I am not paranoid, and if you write that I am paranoid, I will personally sue the *New York Times.*
REX REED

• • •

If my film makes one more person miserable, I'll feel I've done my job.
WOODY ALLEN

• • •

We're talking midlife crisis here. I miss my youth. I've got taxes to pay, I've got hemorrhoids, I don't have any real estate, I've got kids, and they got problems, and I'm nervous about the future.
ABBIE HOFFMAN

• • •

I'm spending about $600 a week talking to my analyst. I guess that's the price of success.
ROBERT DE N1RO

• • •

I occasionally have an anti-Roth reader in mind. I think, "How he is going to hate this!" That can be just the encouragement I need.
PHILIP ROTH

• • •

New York society has not taken to our literature. New York publishes it, criticizes it, and circulates it, but I doubt if New York society much reads it or cares for it, and New York is therefore by no means the literary centre that Boston once was.
WILLIAM DEAN HOWELLS, *LITERATURE AND LIFE*

• • •

Any real New Yorker is a you-name-it-we-have-it-snob . . . and his heart burns with sympathy for the millions of unfortunates who through misfortune, misguidedness, or pure stupidity live anywhere else in the world.
RUSSELL LYNES

• • •

You are an idiot . . . . You are in the presence of one of the great woman scholars of your time, and you behave like an ass, and you're gonna know about it when you're fifty years old. Eat my socks!
CAMILLE PAGLIA, DURING A 1992 VISIT TO PRINCETON UNIVERSITY

• • •

Tree is the number between two and four. *Jeintz* is the name of the New York professional football team. A *fit* is a bottle measuring seven ounces less than a quart. This exotic tongue has no relationship to any of the approved languages at the United Nations, and is only slightly less difficult to master than Urdu.
FLETCHER KNEBEL

• • •

If I didn't get along with people, I just spent time by myself painting. And I didn't get along with people a lot.
JULIAN SCHNABEL

• • •

If I ever had to practice cannibalism, I might manage if there were enough tarragon around.
JAMES BEARD

• • •

It's a place where everyone will stop watching a championship fight to look at an usher giving a drunk the bum's rush.
DAMON RUNYON, ON NEW YORK

• • •

Can we talk?
JOAN RIVERS

• • •

Spoken Like a True New Yorker

It is ridiculous to set a detective story in New York City. New York City is itself a detective story.
AGATHA CHRISTIE

• • •

Living in New York is like being at some terrible late-night party. You're tired, you've had a headache since you arrived, but you can't leave because then you'd miss the party.
SIMON HOGGART

• • •

There is a love-hate relationship between New York and the rest of the country, but New York is unarguably the city that sets the standards, the city in which all who have anything to do with the arts dream of working and succeeding.
HAROLD SCHONBERG

• • •

Only real New Yorkers can find their way around in the subway. If just anybody could find his way around in the subway, there wouldn't be any distinction in being a real New Yorker except talking funny.
CALVIN TRILLIN, *WITH ALL DISRESPECT: MORE UNCIVIL LIBERTIES*

• • •

New York is the biggest collection of villages in the world.
ALISTAIR COOKE

• • •

A car is useless in New York, essential everywhere else. The
same with good manners.
MIGNON MCLAUGHLIN

• • •

Robinson Crusoe, the self-sufficient man, could not have
lived in New York City.
WALTER LIPPMANN

• • •

The true New Yorker secretly believes that people living
anywhere else have to be, in some sense, kidding.
JOHN UPDIKE

• • •

Sometimes I get bored riding down the beautiful streets of L.A. I know it sounds crazy, but I just want to go to New York and see people suffer.
DONNA SUMMER

• • •

People in New York love to tell you how exhausted they are. Then they fall apart when someone says, "Yeah, you look pretty tired."
DAVID SEDARIS, *ME TALK PRETTY ONE DAY*

• • •

New York is a universe: true New Yorkers might suspect the existence of other places, but do not quite believe in them.
ANDREI CODRESCU, *HAIL BABYLON!*

• • •

New York is one of man's greatest achievements.
EDWARD ROBB ELLIS, *THE EPIC OF NEW YORK CITY: A NARRATIVE HISTORY*

• • •

If I'd lived in Roman times, I'd have lived in Rome. Where else? Today America is the Roman Empire and New York is Rome itself.
JOHN LENNON, *JOHN LENNON IN HIS OWN WORDS*

• • •

New York is hell. It is the place where all the negativisms of capitalism converge and blossom.
DOREATHA D. MBALIA, *TONI MORRISON'S DEVELOPING CLASS CONSCIOUSNESS*

• • •

To me, New York is like a bitch of a woman, she's too much to handle, and I don't admire her lifestyle.
DANIELLE STEEL, *GOING HOME*

• • •

There are some who would say with passion that the only real advantage of living in New York is that all its residents ascend to heaven directly after their deaths, having served their full term in purgatory right on Manhattan island.
ALEXANDER KLEIN, *EMPIRE CITY: A TREASURY OF NEW YORK*

• • •

New York is appalling, fantastically charmless and
elaborately dire.
HENRY JAMES, *SELECTED LETTERS OF HENRY JAMES*

• • •

There is little in New York that does not spring from money.
It is not a town of ideas; it is not even a town of causes. But
what issues out of money is often extremely brilliant.
H. L. MENCKEN, *A SECOND MENCKEN
CHRESTOMATHY*

• • •

In a state like Minnesota or Wisconsin you can be poor and
still feel some sense of dignity if you work hard and live
fairly cleanly and you keep your eye on the future. But here
in New York it seemed as if when you're poor you're just
poor. And that means you're nobody. Really nobody.
ROBERT M. PIRSIG, *LILA: AN INQUIRY INTO MORALS*

• • •

New York was a bacchanal of the rich and obnoxious,
a Falstaffian brew of hedonism and material excess: no
boundaries, no breaks—just high octane, high speed,
all the time.
JILL KARGMAN, *THE EX-MRS. HEDGEFUND*

• • •

Here we are Marv. New York City, the land of opportunity.
HARRY, *HOME ALONE 2: LOST IN NEW YORK*

• • •

This is New York City. The only happy endings are in
Chinatown.
BETH, *THE GOOD GUY*

• • •

Chapter One. He was as tough and romantic as the city he
loved. Behind his black-rimmed glasses was the coiled sexual
power of a jungle cat. Oh, I love this. New York was his
town, and it always would be.
ISAAC DAVIS, *MANHATTAN*

• • •

New York is an arrogant city; it has always wanted to be all
things to all people, and a surprising amount of the time it
has succeeded. It has always been a city of commerce, and
the values of commerce have tended to supercede other
values. There is no pretense here of excessive gentility, and
the rush was always to the new, the large, the prosperous, the
fashionable.
PAUL GOLDBERGER

• • •

You come to New York to find the ambiance that will evoke your best. You do not necessarily know precisely what that might be, but you come to New York to discover it.
DR. JAMES HILLMAN

• • •

No one as yet had approached the management of New York in a proper spirit; that is to say, regarding it as the shiftless outcome of squalid barbarism and reckless extravagance. No one is likely to do so, because reflections on the long narrow pig-trough are construed as malevolent attacks against the spirit and majesty of the American people, and lead to angry comparisons.
RUDYARD KIPLING

• • •

As a city, New York moves in the forefront of today's great trend of great cities toward neurosis. She is confused, self-pitying, helpless and dependent.
JOHN LARDNER

• • •

A person who speaks good English in New York sounds like
a foreigner.
JACKIE MASON

• • •

Unfortunately there are still people in other areas who regard
New York City not as a part of the United States, but as a sort
of excrescence fastened to our Eastern shore and peopled by
the less venturesome waves of foreigners who failed to go
West to the genuine American frontier.
ROBERT MOSES

• • •

I love New York City, the reason I live in New York City
is it's the loudest city on the planet Earth. It's so loud I
never have to listen to any of the shit that's going on in my
head. It's really loud, they literally have guys come with
jackhammers and they drill the streets and just leave cones
in front of your apartment and you don't even know why.
Garbage men come they don't even pick up the garbage they
just bang the cans together.
LEWIS BLACK, *THE WHITE ALBUM*

• • •

PART SEVEN

Bronx Cheers and Other Sports News

Some kids want to join the circus . . . others want to be big-league baseball players . . . . When I came to the Yankees I got to do both.
GRAIG NETTLES, NEW YORK YANKEES

• • •

Does football keep you from growing up? Oh, my God, yes! One hundred per cent, yes! I've even heard guys who I thought had no minds at all admit that.
DAVID KNIGHT, NEW YORK JETS

• • •

There is no room in baseball for discrimination. It is our national pastime and a game for all.
LOU GEHRIG

• • •

The highest prize in a world of men is the most beautiful woman available on your arm and living there in her heart loyal to you.
NORMAN MAILER, ON JOE DIMAGGIO'S MARRIAGE TO MARILYN MONROE

• • •

When we won the league championship, all the married guys on the club had to thank their wives for putting up with all the stress and strain all season. I had to thank all the single broads in New York.
JOE NAMATH

• • •

First date, July 30, 1966. I still have the actual ticket stubs. Mets game. I didn't even have a driver's license. I had a double date with a guy named Eddie Cohen. And it was Casey Stengel's 75th birthday, and Eddie had four seats. So I said to [Janice], "You want to go?" she said, "Sure."
BILLY CRYSTAL, ON HIS FIRST DATE WITH JANICE GOLDFINGER, NOW HIS WIFE

• • •

Sure I played, did you think I was born at the age of 70 sitting in a dugout trying to manage guys like you?
CASEY STENGEL, WHEN ASKED BY MICKEY MANTLE IF HE HAD EVER PLAYED BALL

• • •

Till I was thirteen, I thought my name was "shut up."
JOE NAMATH

• • •

No one had ever been booed at a church's Communion breakfast before but they started howling at me as soon as they found out I was filling in for Joe DiMaggio.
PHIL RIZZUTO

• • •

It gets late early out there.
YOGI BERRA, ON THE COMING OF FALL AT YANKEE STADIUM

• • •

The team has come along slow but fast.
CASEY STENGEL

• • •

Your brain commands your body to "Run forward! Bend!
Scoop up the ball! Peg it to the infield! Then your body says,
"who, me?"
JOE DIMAGGIO

• • •

Pitching is the art of instilling fear.
SANDY KOUFAX

• • •

That's why no boy from a rich family ever made the
big leagues.
JOE DIMAGGIO

• • •

If he could cook, I'd marry him.
LEO DUROCHER, ON WILLIE MAYS

• • •

New Yorkers love it when you spill your guts out there. Spill
your guts at Wimbledon and they make you stop and
clean it up.
JIMMY CONNORS

• • •

You are the pits of the world! Vultures! Trash!
JOHN MCENROE, TO FANS, UMPIRES, AND
REPORTERS AT WIMBELDON

• • •

I wanted to kill him. I like him but I wanted to kill him.
ROCKY GRAZIANO, AFTER KNOCKING TONY ZALE
OUT IN THE SIXTH

• • •

Everything you read about George Steinbrenner is true.
That's the problem.
DAVE WIINFIELD

• • •

Winning means everything! You show me a good loser and
I'll show you a loser.
GEORGE STEINBRENNER

• • •

The nice guys are all over there. In seventh place.
LEO DUROCHER, REFERRING TO THE LAST-PLACE NY
GIANTS

• • •

I was there when the flannel turned to double knit.
TOM SEAVER

• • •

Yells for the Mets were also yells for ourselves, a wry, half-understood recognition that there is more Met than Yankee in everyone of us.
ROGER ANGELL, *ONCE MORE AROUND THE PARK*

• • •

Baseball people are generally allergic to new ideas . . . numbers on uniforms . . . spikes on a new pair of shoes. But they will [get together] eventually. They are bound to.
BRANCH RICKEY, GENERAL MANAGER, BROOKLYN DODGERS, ON THE INTEGRATION OF BASEBALL

• • •

There I was the black grandson of a slave, son of a black sharecropper, part of a historic occasion, a symbolic hero to my people . . . [but] I must tell you that it was Mr. Rickey's drama, and that I was only a principal actor.
JACKIE ROBINSON

• • •

I want a ballplayer with guts enough not to fight back.
You will symbolize a crucial cause. One incident, just one
incident, can set it back 20 years.
BRANCH RICKEY, TO JACKIE ROBINSON

• • •

Pro football is like nuclear warfare. There are no winners,
only survivors.
FRANK GIFFORD

• • •

There are three things you can do in a baseball game. You
can win, or you can lose, or it can rain.
CASEY STENGEL

• • •

My greatest strength is that I have no weaknesses.
JOHN MCENROE

• • •

All the time he's boxing he's thinking. All the time he was
thinking, I was hitting him.
JACK DEMPSEY, ON HIS FIGHT WITH BENNY
LEONARD

• • •

If you lose you're going to be fired, and if you win you only put off the day you're going to be fired.
LEO DUROCHER

• • •

It ain't over till it's over.
YOGI BERRA

• • •

I love New York. A part of me will always be here. What can I say.
LATRELL SPREWELL

• • •

You take a team with twenty-five assholes and I'll show you a pennant. I'll show you the New York Yankees.
BILL 'SPACEMAN' LEE

• • •

Hating the New York Yankees is as American as apple pie, unwed mothers and cheating on your income tax.
MIKE ROYKO

• • •

Rooting for the Yankees is like rooting for the house in
blackjack.
ADAM MORROW, QUOTED IN BILL SIMMONS,
"LETTERS FROM THE NATION," 20 OCTOBER 2003

• • •

I think my favorite sport in the Olympics is the one in which
you make your way through the snow, you stop, you shoot
a gun, and then you continue on. In most of the world, it is
known as the biathlon, except in New York City, where it is
known as winter.
MICHAEL VENTRE, *L.A. DAILY NEWS*

• • •

I come from New York, where if you fall down they pick you
up by your wallet.
AL MCGUIRE

PART EIGHT

• • •

The Day the World Trade Center Fell

She said, "Oh, God, please save me," her friend said, clinging to a picture of her friend. "She was screaming that she was trapped and couldn't get out. She said, 'I don't know what to do, I'm coughing, the heat is coming. I need water. I need water.'" And the phone dropped.
ANONYMOUS

• • •

I was in a lot of pain, and burned all over. Nobody had any idea what was going to happen to the buildings. So they were letting all of the people who were hurt go through. Everybody was helping each other.
MANU DHINGRA

• • •

His family is haunted by eerie signs of possible life. Rizzo's pager, which is with him, keeps receiving messages. So they page him and page him, hoping that rescuers will hear the signal from under the rubble.
LYNN JORDAL MARTIN, FOX NEWS

• • •

Let those who say that we must understand the reasons for terrorism come with me to the thousands of funerals we are having in New York City and explain those insane, maniacal reasons to the children who will grow up without fathers and mothers, to the parents who have had their children ripped from them for no reason at all.
RUDOLPH W. GIULIANI

• • •

The last time anyone saw Ganci, the mayor said, he had just ordered the men in his command post to move north to safety. Ganci, himself, then turned back into the disaster area to check on more firefighters. "I am always amazed at how these men walk into fires, when the rest of us run from them," he said.

SALLY JENKINS, THE *WASHINGTON POST*

• • •

I weep and mourn with America. I wish I could comfort every single family whose lives have been affected.

GEORGE W. BUSH

• • •

Everybody called her "Grammy," but her name was Thelma Cuccinello, and she was seventy-one. . . . "I was the last one to see her," [her daughter Cheryl] O'Brien said. "I got to kiss her and say 'I love you' and 'Have a nice trip.' "

CHRISTY OGLESBY, CNN

• • •

You never had to see her to know that she was in a room. You just knew her laugh. She always found a reason to laugh.
BRIAN HULL, ON HIS FRIEND, VALERIE SILVER ELLIS, THE *NEW YORK TIMES*

• • •

What do I tell the pilot to do?
BARBARA OLSON, CNN COMMENTATOR, IN HER LAST WORDS TO HER HUSBAND TED, THE U.S. SOLICITOR GENERAL

• • •

It really came home when I saw guys go in those buildings, and the number that didn't come out . . .
CECIL PULLIAM

• • •

I really believe that if they sent them to hell they would put it out. The World Trade Center collapse was worse than hell.
RUSSELL BEST, CREATOR OF A REALITY TV SHOW ABOUT FIREFIGHTERS CALLED *THE BRAVEST*

• • •

He said, "I want you to know I love you very much, and I'm calling you from the plane. We've been taken over."
ALICE HOGLAN, ON HER SON, MARK BINGHAM, KILLED ON UNITED AIRLINES FLIGHT 93

• • •

I'm on the plane that's been hijacked . . . there's three of us who are going to do something about it.
THOMAS BURNETT JR., TO HIS WIFE FROM UNITED AIRLINES FLIGHT 93

• • •

Let's roll.
TODD BEAMER, AS HE AND OTHER PASSENGERS ON UNITED AIRLINES FLIGHT 93 STRUCK BACK AGAINST THE TERRORISTS

• • •

They are the names of passengers who defied their murderers and prevented the murder of others on the ground. They are the names of men and women who wore the uniform of the United States and died at their posts. They are the names of rescuers whom death found running up the stairs to rescue others.
GEORGE W. BUSH

• • •

The children are devastated. They keep asking every night, "Where's Daddy? Well, Mommy, we watched *Cast Away*. He came back after four years, so maybe Daddy will come back."
ANNE WODENSHEK

• • •

We were asked as children what we wanted to be when we were older and we would answer, "A fireman, a policeman." Today as adults, we again answer, "We want to be like them."
RABBI JOSEPH POTASNIK, FDNY CHAPLAIN, AT THE PRAYER SERVICE AT YANKEE STADIUM

• • •

Rescuers would often arrive to eat and, exhausted, lay their heads on the table to sleep. When they awoke they'd use the bathroom to wash their faces and go back out.
KURT GENDEN, OF THE REGENT HOTEL ON WALL STREET

• • •

We decided to make this for you because peanut butter and jelly sticks together like you guys have stuck together to help America.
A LETTER FROM STUDENTS AT SYLVIA CIRCLE ELEMENTARY SCHOOL IN ROCK HILL, SOUTH CAROLINA

• • •

. . . a thirteen-year-old boy named Cameron, whose brother worked on the l04th floor of one of the towers. U.S. News & World Report reported that after the collapse of the building, Cameron called his brother's cell phone, which was still taking messages. "He just wanted to talk to him one last time," said his father.
JON KYL, U.S. SENATOR

• • •

I'm a loving guy. And I am also someone, however, who's got a job to do and I intend to do it. And this is a terrible moment.
GEORGE W. BUSH

• • •

"Have you seen . . . ?" begins each flyer photocopied and pasted on dozens of walls of hope around the city. Someone's father, someone's sister. Below each picture are the minutae of their existence—every mole, every piece of jewelery, every scar. Perhaps they are injured and unconscious in some hospital, or one of the John or Jane Does.
MICHELE MANDEL, THE *CALGARY SUN*

• • •

The evidence of terrorism's brutality and inhumanity, of its contempt for life and its contempt for peace, is lying beneath the rubble of the World Trade Center less than two miles from where we meet today. Look at that destruction, that massive, senseless, cruel loss of human life, and then I ask you to look in your own hearts and recognize that there is no room for neutrality on the issue of terrorism.
RUDOLPH W. GIULIANI, IN AN ADDRESS TO THE UN

• • •

Now we understand much more clearly, why people from all over the world want to come to New York and to America. It's called freedom.
RUDOLPH W. GIULIANI

• • •

Today, we come together to confess our need of God. Those perpetrators who took us on to tear us apart, it has worked the other way. It has backfired; it has brought us together.
BILLY GRAHAM, AT THE PRAYER SERVICE AT THE NATIONAL CATHEDRAL

• • •

Close to home, a desire to triumph over evil led Continental Airlines gate agent Susan Golden to reach out to travelers marooned at Hartsfield. She took eighteen of them to her house, served them pizza and found them places to sleep. "There's too much goodness in the world to let darkness overcome us," she said.
THE *ATLANTA CONSTITUTION*

• • •

At a time like this, the only saving grace is our common humanity and decency.
JEAN CHRETIEN, CANADIAN PRIME MINISTER

• • •

After George Washington was inaugurated the first President of the United States, in New York City, he walked to St. Paul's, and he kneeled down to pray. The pew where he worshipped is still there. For the past twenty-five years, the chapel stood directly in the shadow of the World Trade Center Towers. When the Towers fell, more than a dozen modern buildings were destroyed and damaged. Yet somehow, amid all the destruction and devastation, St. Paul's Chapel still stands, without so much as a broken window.
RUDOLPH W. GIULIANI, AT THE CITYWIDE PRAYER SERVICE AT YANKEE STADIUM

• • •

If I know Andrew, he stopped to help somebody . . . . I don't want to think about what happened to him, but he's just not here.
ERICA ZUCKER, ABOUT HER HUSBAND, ANDREW

• • •

All it's done is made both children very strong and very determined in what they've set out to do. They're not going to let this setback stop them from the dreams they and their father had.
SARAH TAYLOR, ON HER HUSBAND, DONNIE, THE *NEW YORK TIMES*

• • •

If the events of September 11, 2001, have proven anything, it's that the terrorists can attack us, but they can't take away what makes us American—our freedom, our liberty, our civil rights. No, only Attorney General John Ashcroft can do that.
JON STEWART

• • •

After September 11th, nations from across the globe offered their generous assistance to the people of New York. And whenever our friends around the world need our assistance, New York is there.
GEORGE E. PATAKI

• • •

I am more of a New Yorker than ever and just actually, sometimes I fantasize about living somewhere else, where it's maybe not quite so crowded or stressful, blah, blah, blah and after September 11th, I guess I could just not imagine living anywhere else.
SIGOURNEY WEAVER

• • •

The Day the World Trade Center Fell

I am one of the 11.5 percent of New Yorkers who remain
traumatized by the events of September 11.
LANFORD WILSON

• • •

The city is going to survive, we are going to get through it,
It's going to be a very, very difficult time. I don't think we yet
know the pain that we're going to feel when we find out who
we lost, but the thing we have to focus on now is getting this
city through this, and surviving and being stronger for it.
RUDOLPH GIULIANI

• • •

In the context of September 11, there were so many that lost their
lives that—how do you single out one person? There were so
many acts of heroism that day from so many people, whether it
be firemen and police officers in New York and our agents also.
ROBERT MUELLER

• • •

I was here on 9/11 in high school, so God bless the fire
department. I'm usually a jackass when they tell me I can't set
the piano on fire. So, this is me being a nerd to the town I love.
LADY GAGA BANNED FROM USING PYROTECHNICS
AT A CONCERT / FEBRUARY 23, 2011

• • •

INDEX